The Spiritual Evolution of a Mystic

As Directed by Ramana Maharshi, Jesus,
Koot Hoomi, and Other Ascended Masters

Renee M. Krushel

iUniverse, Inc.
New York   Bloomington

The Spiritual Evolution of a Mystic

iUniverse books may be ordered through booksellers or by contacting:

iUniverse
1663 Liberty Drive
Bloomington, IN 47403
www.iuniverse.com
1-800-Authors (1-800-288-4677)

Because of the dynamic nature of the Internet, any Web addresses or links contained in this book may have changed since publication and may no longer be valid. The views expressed in this work are solely those of the author and do not necessarily reflect the views of the publisher, and the publisher hereby disclaims any responsibility for them.

ISBN: 978-1-4502-6907-0 (sc)
ISBN: 978-1-4502-6908-7 (hc)
ISBN: 978-1-4502-6909-4 (ebook)

Printed in the United States of America

iUniverse rev. date: 12/09/2010

Dedication

To my ascended masters, who have graced me with their attention, guidance, and love.

Acknowledgments

I am exceedingly grateful for my daughter's time-consuming contribution of formatting and drawing the images, as well as for her patience and perseverance in preparing the manuscript for publication.

My gratitude also flows to Carol B. Pearson for editing the notes, to Jeanice Uhrich Lott for editing the manuscript, and to my dear friend Margaret Stanicci for introducing me to meditation.

Contents

Introduction

The masters are anxious to get this information out. They have told me that there will be a "soon-to-come cataclysmic assault on the lower vehicles of humanity," and that "some will survive only with the help of disciples; others will be eliminated." As a disciple, I trust that this book will promote the shift from self-consciousness to spiritual consciousness, a shift that is required if we hope to survive. The messages received from ascended masters were instructions for the evolution of my consciousness as an example to others who are willing to apply the instructions to their own lives.

> During a man's whole life, impressions of a higher
> order than those provided by life may become
> embodied in him. **Mankind is a living medium out
> of which something can—and must—be born.**[1]

When my mystical experiences began over forty years ago, I started keeping a journal. This book includes chronological journal entries, some personal history, the results of my research in many fields, and quotations from other mystics as well as ones from those who have studied them, but most importantly, it contains the guidance and information received from ascended masters and guides. The twenty-seven chapters cover the years from 1968 to 2010.

Many of the journal entries are stranger than fiction, but they are written as they happened, without embellishment.

To quote Rumi, "I am not saying these things to appear visionary and spiritual. I have seen things happen in ways I cannot express."[2]

Be skeptical. I was, but I kept an open mind, too. Skeptics should remain open and not disallow something just because it does not fit their picture of reality. The five senses are very poor interpreters of nonlinear, nonmaterialistic reality.

Because quotations interspersed between narrative passages are seldom read, I have taken the liberty of emboldening words that are especially relevant, amplifying my experiences.

If you get nothing else from this book, you will surely benefit from the exceptionally important instructions and information given to me by the ascended masters.

After years of journaling, researching, and studying without any thought of writing a book, please accept my apologies for any misquotes, any inadvertent failures to quote, quotes that lack page numbers, publishers, or years of publication.

I have recorded the master's transmissions to the best of my ability.

Chapter One
Introduction to Mysticism

Mystical experiences are intuitive and ineffable. Describing them is like describing love to someone who has never been in love. Despite this difficulty, I do my best to tell a story for the following reason:

> Stories exist to be exchanged. They are the currency of human growth. The exchange of story is at the heart of sacred psychology.[1]

Most mystics are closeted. They don't tell their stories, because they are not willing to face the scorn and disdain of others who believe that the reductive materialistic reality of our senses is the only reality. Mystics have been ridiculed and censored by society. Many have been persecuted or put to death for speaking of a transcendent reality, and paradoxically, some of the executed have later been canonized by the Roman Catholic Church. Today, while fear of ridicule may still persist, mystics sense an urgency that requires them to make these experiences public.

For many years attending Manly Palmer Hall's Sunday lectures at the Philosophical Research Society in Los Angeles was the highlight of my week. His portrayal of the mystical life was revelatory. The following is from my notes of his lectures, and from a printed lecture listed in the endnotes.

Mystics are the pioneers of the spiritual world
and society has no right to deny validity to their
discoveries. Transcending the boundaries of normal
physical life, the mystical life is the victory of the eye
single over the two eyes of the outward body. The
mystic transforms the body into an instrument for the
use of soul power. A mystical experience is the internal
eye bringing a new and fuller meaning to external
things, the transformation of knowledge into what
might be termed archetypal wisdom, the revelation
of the principles behind the commonplace, the
mysterious power that transforms the beauty of the
rose into a symbol of universal beauty, the enrichment
of every act. As the mystic reaches a higher level of
things, the tendency is for mystical attainments to
appear symbolically. This is another level and involves
the individual interpreting things according to their
internals instead of their externals.[2]

There is a close correspondence between the timeless, spaceless, unified, informational field experienced by mystics and that described and labeled by cutting-edge scientists and thinkers. This unified field is akin to David Bohm's implicate order, Rupert Sheldrake's morphogenic field, Ervin Laszo's psi or zero-point energy field, Teilhard de Chardin's noosphere, and Aurobindo's supramental.

Physicists are verifying what mystics of all ages have said—that the universe is a unity, that everything is connected, and that the world cannot be analyzed into separate and independently existing parts. Non-locality and quantum entanglement suggest that spatially separated systems influence one another, indicating that there is some connection between systems that are physically separated.

In the sixties, LSD and other hallucinogens were used to induce altered states of consciousness. Today, new immersive media technologies offer mystical-like interactive experiences.

There are many ways to induce altered states, none of which I used; my mysticism commenced spontaneously in 1968, shortly after I began to meditate.

True knowledge and description must be left to
the language of the mystic's direct and concrete
experience.[3]

My approach to mysticism has always been skeptical and pragmatic,
initially doubted, later researched in an attempt at corroboration and
understanding, and finally accepted.

Chapter Two
Beginnings

The culmination of the soul's journey of awakening
is not just returning to its original state. Instead, it
is how the soul has evolved through its passage on
earth…and the unique way each soul's unfoldment
has contributed to the evolution of the Universe itself.
Pir Vilayat Inayat Khan

March 1968

For most of the first eight years of my life, I was confused by being
moved from one reluctant relative to another. From time to time,
I lived with my mother and sometimes my father, whom I did not
remember back then. When I was twenty-three, in response to my
request, my mother arranged a meeting with him. I later learned from
him that he had been coerced into remarrying her in order to have his
daughter back in his life.

At eight, I was sexually abused repeatedly by a family member.
At nineteen, I married an abusive alcoholic, became pregnant on my
wedding night, and gave birth to a daughter nine months later. After
five years of verbal abuse, my focus moved to two things: education
and escape. Thirteen years later, with a bachelor's degree and a teaching
credential in one hand and a suitcase in the other, my daughter and
I walked away. My second marriage was troublesome, but love and

several shared mystical experiences kept us together for forty-one years until his death.

To say that my life changed when I began meditating in 1968 would be an understatement. In fact, I became a different person. The paranormal experiences started almost immediately, scaring but not deterring me. Confused by voices and visions, a lifelong exploration and a self-imposed study program commenced and took me in many directions. I studied psychology, philosophy, metaphysics, mysticism, mythology, science, and anything else that I thought might help me comprehend what was happening. Assurances of my sanity came from many books.

Mysticism by Evelyn Underhill and *Religions, Values, and Peak Experiences* by Abraham Maslow helped the most. Claudio Naranjo's *The One Quest*, *Varieties of Religious Experience* by William James, and *Cosmic Consciousness* by Richard Bucke helped me to accept my mysticism, which was a blessing in disguise. Although my studies taught me much, without the guidance and grace of my later-to-be discovered ascended masters and guides, I would never have found the evolutionary path that exists in a realm beyond the intellect.

> It is entirely possible that we are bathed and
> surrounded by the transcendent and yet have not
> tuned it in.[1]

> To know yourself you need not go to any book, to any
> priest, to any psychologist. The treasure lies within.[2]

To know yourself and to recognize that the treasure lies within as Krishnamurti tells us, you will probably need a lifetime of introspection and some assurance from others.

Like a teenager secretly writing in a diary, I began recording my experiences in journals. The following are some of my entries.

March 1968

As we waited to be introduced to the parents on a "back to school" night, I asked the teacher beside me why I never saw her in the cafeteria at lunchtime. Her concise response was the following: "I meditate." The word "meditate" exploded in my brain like fireworks on the Fourth of July, and I knew that whatever it was, I had to learn how to do it. I asked her if she would teach me to meditate. She said she would and told me to come to her classroom the following day. The next day as I sat with her, she instructed, "Sit with your back straight, close your eyes, take several deep breaths, and don't think." Within the first ten minutes of meditation, I had visions of scintillating violet-colored swirls enveloping a large lustrous pearl, and my hands and head became very hot. My instructor's response to my experience was quite shocking. She simply said, "You're probably going to be a healer." After several weeks, she pushed me out of the nest, assuring me that I was ready to fly solo.

It took some time to strengthen my wings, but today, I received my first message: *Create and mold. It is important to be creative. I-Thou create; I-you consume.* It was stunning to be addressed without audition by an entity without a visible body.

> Our degree of consciousness limits what we see, if
> extended we could see another range of reality.[3]

During the next month, I began receiving longer telepathic messages:

> *Love is wisdom. Love is unity. What you seek*
> *is within. Change will take place without effort;*
> *the answers will come through you and the word*
> *"balance."*

Sitting in meditation seemed too easy, so I researched and tried many different techniques. Each experiment was followed by the following: *That is not your way.* Evidently, my way was simply sitting without thought but remaining receptively alert.

> To meet everything and everyone through stillness
> instead of mental noise is the greatest gift you can
> offer to the universe.[4]

Early one evening, a command came to me: *Baptize thyself.* Puzzled and curious, I filled the bathtub, submerged myself, and emerged waterlogged but purified.

April 1968

This morning as I was meditating I received this message.

> *God is love. God is in you. Human suffering is the result of free will. Your purpose is to love, sacrifice, and serve. You exist to co-create.*

After many years of searching and not finding a religion that seemed right for me, I became agnostic, so hearing about God was definitely unforeseen.

But today, hearing the words God and "co-create" has great significance. To fulfill our purpose on this planet, we must co-create a new level of consciousness that can solve our mounting problems. Was it Einstein who stated, "You can't solve a problem with the same consciousness that created it?"

A larger-than-life nebulous entity appeared in my bedroom tonight to admonish me for allowing my husband's passive aggressive behavior to depress me.

> *It doesn't matter where you are; it matters that you manifest God. Rise up out of material existence and express me. I am the Word, the Law. Come up out of the mud and purify yourself for my service. Rise up. Implore me to tell you about yourself. Until you see yourself, you will not see me.*
>
> *Suffer your outrageous fortune. Let him be. Expect nothing. Express God. Stop playing in*

the mud. Mud pulls and clings; it sucks you down into the center of the earth. You are being soiled by your concern for the material. Tell him to pray, no more, no less. Move on. You have work to do. In your foolish exuberance, you want to save the world. Beware of fanaticism, even in the family. Be ye perfect. Ask nothing of man. Expect nothing and you will not be disappointed. Though you persecute me, I will not accuse you. Forgive him; he knows not. He does the best he can. Remove yourself beyond his reach. Guard your thoughts—where your thoughts are, there you are also. Suffer and abide with me. The advice of men is faulty. Only through divine revelation will the truth be known. Each man sounds a note; together, you make music.

In a dream, I dropped a large cake that appeared to be white; however, it was dark inside. Was I the cake, externally light and internally dark? Was it a foreboding? Was it what Jung called the shadow?

A high-pitched note caught my attention.

Balance, harmony, love. Free yourself from attachments and the fears that inhibit your ability to love and create. Be present in each moment.

I had no idea what "be present in each moment" meant. In 1968, even mystic Eckhart Tolle did not know what it meant. He wrote *The Power of Now* after his awakening in 1977.

August 1969

The word "fulcrum" popped into my head. It means, "The support about which a lever turns, or, one that supplies stability for action." The second meaning seems more occultly appropriate.

I received this puzzling message:

> *We can only make it with others. Reversing action never makes things right. One side of something is simply a reflection of the other side.*

Chapter Three
Life after Death

May 1972

I did not believe in the survival of the soul or spirit after death until months after my brother-in-law died. One weekend while my husband and I were painting a fence, Jay called my name over and over again. "Obviously, it's my imagination. He's dead," I told myself. His call persisted for hours. Exhausted from painting and tired of his incessant call, I finally gave in and asked what he wanted. He replied, "Call Mary" referring to his wife. The next day, I called and continued to do so about once a month in response to the same request, never revealing to anyone the promptings from Jay.

One day, I asked, "Why me?"

He replied enigmatically, "Who else?"

As I still pondered his meaning, I contacted each family member to ask, "Have you had any sense of Jay's presence?" No one had, so Jay's reply to my question made perfect sense, for there really was no one else.

One evening I boldly proposed "Since I have been honoring your request will you honor mine and tell me about the other side?"

Almost before I had uttered the last word, the response came. It sounded like Jay, but when my hair stood at attention, I knew it wasn't Jay. "I'll tell you about the other side if you'll allow me to live through you," whispered the voice.

Chilled and quaking with fear, I made the sign of the cross and recited every prayer I had ever learned in Sunday school until I felt safe. That terrifying incident convinced me that humans could be possessed by the dead. Like Goethe's Faust, I had inadvertently almost made a pact with Mephistopheles, the devil.

Jay was becoming a problem. Not only was he opening me to potential possession, but he was manifesting wherever and whenever he wished. The deciding factor came when he appeared in the passenger's seat while I was driving on the freeway. He had to go! That evening, I asked him why he was still earthbound. He confessed that the paralyzing fear he felt, alone in the ambulance at the moment of his death, and his concern for the welfare of Mary and his teenage sons kept him here. (He died of a massive heart attack before the ambulance arrived at the hospital. He was fifty-one years old, when two weeks earlier, he had been told by his doctor that there was nothing wrong with his heart.)

With the bravado of the ignorant, intending to attempt his release, I found myself inside the ambulance. Though I had never seen the inside of an ambulance, I now saw it in great detail, a vision verified as accurate many years later. As I held him tightly in my arms, the heart attack replayed. After I promised him that Mary and "the boys," as we called them, would be fine, I declared, "You're free now!" My sadness turned to joy as he left his body and was catapulted out of the ambulance. Now he would be able to check on his family without my help.

Chapter Four
Enlightenment

May 7, 1972

As I entered the house after attending a two-day seminar on healing, I greeted my husband, who was reading a newspaper, when suddenly my sense of "I" disappeared. There was no self, no body, no space, no time, and no other. In a dimension of pure consciousness, infinite knowledge, and eternal truth, all fear dropped away as the realization of our infinitude dawned on me. Trying to communicate this experience was essentially impossible, because there was no me to experience it—no beginning and no end, only unity, love, and information. Consciousness was omniscient, omnipresent, and all-loving, one with everything. As soon as I attempted to conceptualize the experience, I was back in my body, standing on the same spot, and my husband was still reading the newspaper. The need to understand separated me from the singularity, and the duality of mundane life returned. In perhaps several seconds or minutes, my life was altered at a fundamental level. Before, I had doubted, but now I knew that we are indivisible, infinite centers of universal consciousness. We have always existed and will always exist in some form. I understood what Jesus and other mystics meant when they declared, "The Father and I are one."

For days after this experience, there were moments of clairvoyance, intuition, and a sense of identity with everything: water, minerals, animals, plants, and people. Dreams became insightful. The fragrance of sandalwood, flowers, freshly sawed wood, and the ocean wafted about without their material presence.

> Do you smell the **fragrance of sandalwood**? I can give
> off perfumes at any time.[1]

Now my definition of enlightenment is quite different from what it was years ago. Because I continued studying and evolving, I knew that enlightenment was an evolving process that was never achieved once and for all. Our purpose is to continue to evolve the consciousness of this planet.

> **There is only one in the universe, not two**, and that
> one is consciousness.[2]

> Mystics use the mind to probe a transcendental reality
> not accessible to the instruments of science, a realm
> that is the abode of the **wave aspect of reality**.[3]

Quantum mechanics has proven that all matter has wave-particle potential. Waves become particles when they are observed.

> In, "vision" or "union," the mind is somehow
> privileged to experience itself as the eternal
> Consciousness from which the entire universe is
> projected.[4]

> Enlightenment is the realization of oneness with **all
> states** and **all stages** that have evolved so far and that
> are in existence at any given time.[5]

According to my understanding of Ken Wilber's, *states* can be experienced at all *stages* and at any time. A mystical experience can be considered a state. A stage is an achieved evolutionary level. One can experience changes in states of consciousness while one remains at the same stage. For example, a very young child will be at a survival stage of consciousness and still may have high-level, temporary state experiences.

We are in touch with something outside the empirical
realm, a different order of being; we literally have
the experience of **being taken out of time and space**
altogether, and also **out of ourselves,** even out of the
material object that is our body.[6]

During a lecture by Manly P. Hall, my whole body vibrated as he
described Samadhi, because I was able to give my experience a name—
Samadhi or Enlightenment.

Samadhi is essentially **the suspension of the
experience of self-existence.** In Samadhi the mystic
is no longer able to identify himself as a being. He
does not exist any longer because his existence is the
final illusion he has to overcome. There is only one
existence and he is a fragment, a spark of it.[7]

Today I listened to philosopher Ervin Laszlo speak about the
informational field, the Akasha, where everything that ever was is
recorded and can be accessed through meditation or other activities
that allow for transcendent experience.[8]

When the veil of ignorance, which constitutes the ego,
was lifted, it was revealed that my true, underlying
identity is and always has been, the one all pervading
consciousness that is the source and substratum of all
that exists.[9]

That inseparable **quantum interconnectedness** of the
whole universe **is the fundamental reality.**[10]

I felt that nothing existed and in their stead
I perceived a boundless effulgent **ocean of
intelligence.**[11]

The mystic is no longer able to identify himself as a

being because there is a **suspension of the experience of self-existence.**[12]

Individuality itself seemed to dissolve and fade away into boundless being, and this not a confused state but the clearer, the surest of the sure, utterly beyond words—where death was an almost laughable impossibility—**the loss of personality** (if so it were) seeming no extinction, but **the only true life.**[13]

The above quotes are included to further describe and illustrate my experience of enlightenment or Samadhi from the perspective of the mystic and the physicist.

February 1973

During a three-part dream, the symbols presented were also explained.

1. I was obsessed with cutting every bit of fat from a piece of meat that was on my plate. When I was satisfied that all that I considered undesirable was gone, so was the piece of meat, which meant, "Taking things apart destroys their integrity."

2. I was about to be gored by a charging bull, and rather than running, I mimicked the movements of a toreador, which meant, "Respond to aggression by stepping aside."

3. When I tried to shoo away a tiger that was in the living room, it menacingly bared its teeth. As I ignored the threat, I confidently walked forward, and it became a purring kitten that I picked up and cuddled, which meant, "Fears are our own creations."

I have been seeing halos or auras all day.

March 1973

The importance of balance was brought to my attention again. In last night's dream, I was walking on high wire.

> The master ... was teaching me the secret of **balanced living.**[14]

> We are doomed by our **unbalanced growth.**[15]

After today's meditation, several days of back pain finally ended.

My sense of taste so intensified that during this evening's meal, every morsel exploded with flavor. Ordinary food became ambrosia, food of the gods.

> And everything that one eats and drinks becomes transformed into blissful **ambrosia.**[16]

The word "suddha" came. (Years later, I read that "suddha" means "pure self.")

Believing that the pinnacle of spirituality, with its uncontainable ecstasy, had been reached, I prayed for death. Fortunately, a wise friend warned, "Praying for death is dangerous," and she convinced me that there was much more of life to be experienced. How foolish it was to think that I had reached the mountaintop—one never does. We are continually evolving with the cosmos.

Chapter Five
Mystical Marriage

August 1973

For several days, the feeling that something unusual was about to happen had me concerned. I prayed, "Please don't let me become one of those born-again Christians." That evening, someone commanded, "*Baptize Thyself.*" Unsettled and somewhat reluctant, I filled the guest bathroom's bathtub with water, because the master suite had an open sleeping/dressing/bathing area and the smaller enclosed bath was more suitable for a baptism. As the warm water engulfed me, a second command directed, "*Adorn thyself as a bride in white.*" Dressed in an almost-white, faded flannel nightgown, the nearest thing to bridal white, I hesitatingly approached the master bedroom. The contents of the room were obscured in a cloudlike, pale blue mist. The only thing that I could see was a radiant figure of light, a man in a long white gown standing beside my dressing table. Terrified and about to scream, he banished my fear and immobilized me. Mesmerized but without doubt, I knew him to be Jesus Christ. Emptied of all that was my "self," I stood frozen as His light body glided toward me. We merged, became one in an all-consuming rapture, and I experienced a moment of blissful, sublimated sex. Utterly fulfilled and in a transcendent daze I glided to my bed, climbed in, and basked in the exalted union until sleep consumed me.

I did not become a born-again Christian; I became the bride of

Christ.

> I sat long enough in fire. Now I am up to my neck in the water of union. Rumi

> The mystical marriage "is the initiation of suprasexual co-creation."[1]

> Whenever anyone is united to Christ, there is a new creature: his old life is over; a new life is already begun.[2]

Some Catholic nuns spoke or wrote of their mystical marriage to Jesus, but they never mentioned a union of bodies. However, I found two descriptions similar to mine, both written by men. They are listed below.

> I saw Him in my house ... among all those everyday things. **He appeared unexpectedly** and became unutterably united and **merged with me** ... and he made me like fire and like light.[3]

> One day, while walking in his favorite grove, meditating on Jesus, he saw coming toward him a man with large beautiful eyes, and serene countenance and fair skin, and he realized that it was Jesus. As they embraced, the form of Jesus merged into his own.[4]

> In the mystical traditions, **soul infusion is linked with the mystical marriage.**[5]

March 1974

Because I felt abandoned by God, I decided to try baptism in desperation. It had worked twice before. With some apprehension, I filled the tub. While in the water, I cried, "Thy will, dear Lord, not mine, I give myself to Thee." Immediately, I perceived an objective view of my despair and recognized it as a creation of my own mind. What a moment ago had seemed very serious now was exceedingly funny, and I laughed and laughed hysterically. I gave myself to God, and ironically, I received Buddha consciousness.

> When I returned to my senses, I began clapping
> my hands together with delight and emitting great
> **whoops of laughter.**[6]

Chapter Six
Different Realities

May 1974

While I was closeting the tricycles after recess, I felt nothing, but a bloody palm alerted me. As I signaled to another teacher, I hurried to the school nurse, who cleaned and bandaged a large V-shaped cut in the palm of my right hand. That evening when my husband asked what had happened, I removed the bandage to show him my wound. Astonished because my hand looked perfect, we examined it with our most powerful magnifying glass and found not even a hint of the cut. After that spontaneous healing, there were others.

Often when a scrape or a cut warranted taking a child to the nurse, the injury was healed by the time we entered her office.

I just received this message from a master:

> *In your Father's house, there are many mansions. Live in your Father's house, not in the worldly hell you call home. Rise up in consciousness despite your suffering. If you share the vibration of the masses, you will be of no use to us. We need you where you are, but recognize that your spirit resides in your Father's*

house, a place of light, love, and knowledge. The door is always open for you to come and go. This is your true home. The table is set. The feast awaits your arrival, but you prefer your world. Soon you will change your preference. Your masters love you and are aware of your comings and goings. Abide with us in faith and love. As the earth becomes increasingly hellish, your light and love will be needed.

How strange that a former agnostic should have become a believer.

June 1974

Drifting in and out of dissimilar levels of consciousness makes living a balanced life difficult.

December 1974

Today, an amorphous, rose-colored presence explained the following:

Everything you need you already have. Disease is imbalance.

These words established peace between my many warring selves.

Today, the vision of a huge pyramid with an eye in the apex bewildered me.

Dreams of white animals and snakes shedding skin seemed to indicate a new birth for me. My name, Renee, means renaissance or rebirth.

White animals play an important role in various

cultures as wise advisors or predictors of the future.[1]

May 1975

During a dream, an ancient master taught me to levitate.

> Scholars who know nothing of the experience of unity postulate some cultural interchange to account for the similarities in the accounts of mystics, or postulate an "archetypal memory" from which identical images arose, it never dawning on them that the **direct knowledge of the one Absolute and its projection of the universe is an actual experience common to all seers at all times.**[2]

When my daughter called to tell me that her father, my first husband, had died, I prayed that his transition would be free of trouble, even though we had been divorced for many years. Instantly, he appeared floating above me, young and vital, and said, "At last, I'm free of that body," and in a flash, he was gone. He died of esophageal cancer, probably as a result of his drinking and smoking.

This morning ethereal music is playing in my head. Pythagoras is usually credited with the concept of "the music of the spheres"; and although he was said to be the only one who could hear it, I also can hear it from time to time.

June 1975

In Siena, Italy, we happened upon a church that displayed the body of Saint Catherine of Siena, or so it seemed.

As the story went, the people of Siena travelled to Rome to bring Catherine home. Unable to do that, they somehow managed to steal parts of her. On their way out of Rome, they were stopped and asked to disclose the contents of a bag that contained Catherine's parts. Miraculously, the bag now only contained rose petals. When they reached Siena, Catherine's head and finger reappeared. She was placed on view as if her body were intact.

I sat in meditation at the back of the church in Siena, sensing that something was about to happen, when my husband interrupted, "We have to move on." Because I was unwilling to leave without buying something from the small shop housed within the church, I purchased a triptych of the saint. We were leaving when the shopkeeper, noticing a priest approaching, snatched the package from my hand and thrust it toward the priest, who perfunctorily made some strange movement with his hands and hurried on.

Weeks later while I was reorganizing my suitcase for our return to California, I opened a small package to see what it contained. A hurricanelike force pushed me backward. In the package was the triptych of Saint Catherine of Siena.

Saint Catherine of Siena was a Dominican nun, a philosopher, and a theologian who tried to unite the papacy, which was split between Italy and France during her time. She died in Rome on April 29, 1380, when she was thirty-three years old. She was proclaimed a doctor of the church in 1970.

Saint Catherine wrote, *"my mind is so full of joy and happiness that I am amazed my soul stays in my body."*[3]

Catherine of Siena had visitations from Christ and what she considered a marriage to Jesus. In visions, she saw a baby in the hands of a priest. She often would smell a strong but sweet aroma, and she had burning sensations at times.[4]

July 1975

This morning I heard:

*You are totally responsible for your experience.
You can't change things by trying. Whatever you
desire to change will persist.*

Chapter Seven
Dark Night of the Soul

November 1975

Since our return from Europe, a deathlike feeling is gripping me, and ordinary consciousness is being siphoned off. I ask, "Is this the dark night of the soul suffered by St. John of the Cross?"

Dark night of the soul is a metaphor used to describe the loneliness and desolation felt when one is separated from God.

> It is necessary to become dead to what has become for
> you your ordinary life.[1]

This morning while I was getting dressed, this inscrutable message entered my consciousness:

> *You've come a long way daughter. I now*
> *claim you. Soon, you shall be picking the lilies*
> *of the field.*

I looked in the Bible to find a reference I vaguely remembered:

> Consider the lilies of the field, how they grow, they
> neither toil nor, neither do they spin.[2]

During our walk that morning, nothing seemed ordinary. The pristine world of nature was vibrantly alive and part of me. Trees nodded their greetings, and the flowers fluoresced just for me. Joyously buoyant, my husband's arm was needed to keep me from rising like a balloon.

I did not seem to be walking on the earth.[3]

December 1975

My consciousness—when it is either awake or dreaming—is lucid, symbolic, and instructive. I float out of my body, and in dreams, I give birth to myself and animals—usually white ones—walk on high wires, and receive prizes and blessings from ascended beings.

January 1976

I dreamt that Christ appeared in a sky awash with kaleidoscopic patterns. The spectacle of animals and insects materializing made me ecstatic but frightened others.

March 1976

The following message came from one of the masters:

> *You have gone too far to turn back. This is a new beginning. No inconsistency can be tolerated without immediate consequences. You will be enabled to advance faster. Praise the Lord; you shall be free of all your worldly desires. When this is accomplished, you will be in a realm that you can't even imagine.*
>
> *The mind records multisensory perceptions*

*of continual nows. It has a record of everything
that was or will be.*

February 1977

EST (Erhard Seminar Training) sponsored a Black Crown ceremony given by the Karmapa of Tibet, and because I had just finished the EST training, I attended the ceremony. As the monks began to chant, I felt a whirling sensation that started at the base of my spine and ended at the throat. My head twitched, and my eyes fluttered. At home, my chin, mouth, and throat became ablaze for several hours. I later realized that my chakras had been activated.

After a long period of passive negativity and depression, the masters told me to resume my volunteerism, which I had begun eight years ago in New York's Foundling Hospital. Consequently, I volunteered at the Los Angeles Children's Hospital yesterday.

March 1977

Another suprising message came:

> *This is a beginning—God is now directing
> your life.*

A sense of impending doom is descending upon me. Does one need to physically die to be reborn?

> Heroes always emerge in a time of dying—of self, of
> social sanctions, of society's forms, of standard-brand
> religions, governments, economics, psychologies and
> relationships.[4]

A golden aura around my head and shoulders is reflected by the mirror before me.

April 10, 1977

— On Easter morning I heard:

> *A mystic is chosen. He must relinquish the world and himself. You must come now!*

"Come where?" I asked.

Once again, I see a large golden glow around my head and shoulders. Is this what young children see when they stare at me and smile? Today, while I was shopping in a department store, I looked up to see a beaming three-year-old girl arrested by what she saw. Her gleeful smile made me feel like a clown in full makeup. The mother, retracing her steps to retrieve her child, tugged, but the girl wouldn't move. As she was pulled away, still beaming, she waved good-bye.

May 1977

While I bathed, I sang, "Praise God from whom all blessings flow. Praise Him all creatures here below. Praise Him above ye heavenly host. Praise Father, Son, and Holy Ghost." A strong current of energy tore through my body. Flames consumed me without burning. The flames then formed a triangle that next arched into a rainbow, and a voice boomed, *The dross has been burnt.*

> **The fire of the body burns away its dross**; and rising
> in a flame of self-surrender, consumes its closed
> microcosm.[5]

Chapter Eight
Past Lives

June 1977

Despite the fact that I did not believe in reincarnation, spontaneous memories of what I presumed to be former lives began to flash in my mind. Hundreds or thousands of years ago, Karim, a moneylender or merchant in Damascus, Syria, was counting coins by candlelight when an intruder entered the room and struck him. The first blow glanced off his head and landed on his left shoulder. Several other blows finished the assault. As the thief was gathering coins, I died in a pool of blood.

In my twenties, I decided to make my own clothing to save money. To facilitate the fitting process, I ordered a body mannequin. When I noticed that the left shoulder blade protruded more than the right did, I checked my back. The mold was indeed accurate. Pain in that part of my body still plagues me. Was that asymmetry and pain a remnant of a former life?

Several weeks after that regression, I found myself regressing again. A harem dancer was entertaining men seated in front of a magnificent building in Agra, India. Years later, during a world tour, I recognized the building. It was not the Taj but almost as grand.

> He who remembers his "births" (origin) and his
> **former lives** … succeeds in freeing himself from
> karmic conditioning: in other words, he becomes
> master of his destiny.[1]

A sudden shock to the head left me with a headache for several days. There was no storm outside, nor was I near any electrical appliance.

> The devotee is gradually conditioned to accept this
> power to work through him as [he] learns to control
> his body [to] accept the **bolts of electricity**.[2]

The electric shock altered my perception: A simple patch of grass became a jungle. Noise became music. The fragrance of flowers followed me. Trees nodded their greetings. Even the ugly seemed beautiful. During this episode, I was Alice in Wonderland, alternating between being very small and very tall.

Each tree in the park had a unique and contented vibration until some of them were marked for elimination. Then, even the unmarked trees withdrew in fear.

During meditation, the simple vision of a five-pointed star induced a state of euphoria that lasted for several days.

While I was attending a conference in Santa Barbara, I joined a group meditation led by Peter Caddy, one of the founders of Findhorn in Scotland. In closing, he had us join hands and send healing energy counterclockwise around the circle. Though I was expecting warm and loving feelings, instead I received the group's accumulated negativity which manifested as pain in my left palm. Unwilling to pass the pain to the next person, the directive came, *"Raise your vibration,"* and the pain dissolved, allowing me to send healing love.

June, 1977

Today we arrived in Damascus, Syria.

Our tour group was walking along a narrow street lined with barrels of spices and other exotic items when I was suddenly overcome with dread. Why was I walking with strange-looking people from another land instead of offering spices for sale from my stall? Brought back to the present by one of my travelling companions, I later wondered if a sudden change in my appearance had elicited the question, "Where are you from?" Before this moment, there had been many opportunities to ask that question.

A memory was triggered as we entered a small museum with mannequins dressed in chadors.

Years ago, before my mysticism surfaced, I decided to paint a self-portrait. The canvas was gessoed, the paints on the pallet, and the mirror in place. With brush in hand, the painting began. The palette shimmered with beautiful colors: however, the color chosen was black, and the brushstrokes were not mine. Mesmerized and unable to resist, I watched as a bystander while an unknown artist painted her self-portrait.

The figureless background and the single figure were both painted black. The only other colors used were touches of white and peach to indicate the glow of a campfire reflected on the face and on the folds of the chador she was wearing. At this time, I had no knowledge of automatic painting, reincarnation, or Islamic culture and religion. The person on the canvas looked like me, but she was not the one I saw in the mirror. Now, more than twenty years later, I am in Damascus, Syria, shifting back and forth in time while a facsimile of the woman who painted her self-portrait is staring back at me through mannequin eyes.

At our next stop, we (women) were asked to don chadors before we entered a mosque. As my current identity was being obscured beneath the black garment, a transformation was in progress, and once again, I became the woman in the painting.

November 1977

Only three months at home since our world tour, another dark night of the soul has engulfed me. I would welcome death only if it brought me to God.

Weeks of despondency finally signaled Kundalini, the little white snake sleeping at the base of my spine, from her long nap. She was winding her way through the chakras, enlivening each as she climbed. Finally, when she reached my head, she turned on a radiant golden light that beamed from my eyes, and I was finally able to shed my despondency like she shed her skin.

This afternoon while my husband was walking our dogs Victoria and Elizabeth in a neighborhood park, I stood against my favorite tree, merging with its vibrations. When I heard shouts, I looked to see two dogs galloping toward me from different directions: one a tiny poodle, the other a huge German shepherd. Although the dogs did not know each other or me, we started exchanging greetings with pats, scratches, and wagging tails when two frightened men reached us. Each said he had never seen his unfriendly dog interacting happily with a stranger. I patted Pierre, the poodle. His eyes rolled back as he became entranced and immobilized for several seconds. We bonded and became buddies. I never saw the German shepherd again.

Years passed, and we lost track of our park friends, both the dogs and the people. Just before Christmas we received an unexpected invitation from Bill and Tom, Pierre's owners. (I hate to think of a dog being owned, but using the word "masters" would be even more offensive to me.) Upon our arrival at the Christmas open house, we were greeted by Bill and Tom, but Pierre was no where to be seen. The house was full of people with whom my husband and I exchanged greetings when out of a darkened room bounded Pierre. He had heard my voice and perhaps smelled me. Our happy reunion was a surprise to all.

December 1977

I finally learned how to raise my vibration from slow and heavy to fast and light, from depression to happiness, a surprising feat when it worked.

We didn't have a Christmas tree, but I was smelling pine.

In Manly Hall's *Occult Anatomy of Man*, he mentions that a sprig of evergreen promises life to those who raise the serpent power.

January 1978

Learning to transform energy has not come easily. A shift from emotional to mental, from mystical to occult is in process.

I heard "You are a point of light within a greater light," and received this poem.

> Dear child of God,
> How delicate are the wings
> that propel you through space to me.
>
> O heavenly specter,
> My heart reaches out to thee.
> Let loose the strings that tie you to earth
> And float with us amongst fleeting forms of fantasy.

My daughter came to visit after an unpleasant divorce. The night after she left, I slept in the guest room. Awakened by a nightmare, what I saw when I turned the lights on was more frightening than the dream. In the room with me were many ugly, troll-like gnomes rollicking about, taunting me with grimaces and gestures, saying nasty things about my daughter. As I slammed the door on my way out, I fled to my own bed and began reading a pamphlet on positive thinking. A flaming eggshell instantly formed around me, and I fell asleep knowing that I was protected. The next morning, I wondered if my daughter's thoughts had brought the gnomes or if they had been attracted to a hand-carved Maltese cross I had purchased from monks in a remote monastery in Syria.

> The **elementals** are in their essential essence **sub-human**. The fact that they can be contacted on the emotional plane is no guarantee that they are on the evolutionary path. On the contrary they are on the **path of involution**, on the downward arc. They are to be found on all planes and the etheric elemental forms—such as the brownies, **gnomes**, and pixies— are well known.[3]

I wore the cross for the next few nights and had dreams of being attacked with knives by my husband and my mother.

Several weeks later, I wore the cross again. This time, it did not attract visible gnomes, but it did attract negative entities that I could not see but could feel. Revolted, I ripped the cross from my neck and threw it across the room. Later, after I had washed it with salt water and dried it in the sun, I was sure it was purified. Several weeks later, I wore the cross again with similar results. I threw it away, though I probably should have taken it to a psychometrist for a reading.

Everything seemed normal at the international conference until I saw a golden halo form around the upper part of the presenter's body. When I quickly glanced around the room to see if anyone else saw it, I soon realized they did not. My eyes returned to the speaker, whose halo had enlarged, and became a featureless body that hovered beside him. Its upper part was golden, its lower part black. When the presenter began chanting in a foreign language, I was able to chant along with him without understanding a word. Before our lunch break when all the presenters were together on a platform, I carefully checked each one, but only he had an etheric double.

For the last session of the conference, I chose to join a guided meditation conducted by Sufi Master Pir Vilayat Inayat Khan, the son of Hazrat Inayat Khan, who introduced Sufism to the United States. When Khan began the meditation, I was fully alert, but at some point, I left while my body remained. After the meditation ended, I became aware of a voice directing someone to move one part of her body at a time. Khan was talking to me. With difficulty, I was able to move my limbs little by little, but it took about as long to fully return to the body as it had taken for the meditation.

Today I heard:

> *Don't run from pain. There is much to learn from your own discomfort. Don't engage in arguments; agree with your opponent. Don't be fooled by appearances; the most ferocious-looking dog might lick your hand. When you try to get rid of the bad, you also destroy the good—both are but two halves of a whole. Flow with life. Don't let circumstances dictate to you.*

Be balanced and harmonic. Fear is the biggest barrier to life. Replace fear with faith. Faith is surrender.

This evening as I meditated several past lives surfaced.

- A naked man wearing a crescent moon on a cord around his neck is being tortured. Heavy wooden rollers are crushing my arms.
- As I listen to a call to prayer from the minaret, I see men wearing white, watching us dance.
- As a Bedouin, I see many tents, a campfire, and camels.

February 1978

One evening, bleary-eyed from reading, I was at the sink splashing water on my face to refresh myself when the mirror reflected a hunchbacked nun. The words "Sister of Charity," a phrase unknown to me at the time, identified her. The habit I was wearing was heavy, but what felt most uncomfortable was the binding around my forehead and the tightly laced shoes. The physical sensations remained for quite a while.

My Methodist Episcopal Sunday-school training amounted to no more than about four years total, evenly separated by five years with no religious training.

Despite the fact that as a child I was told that Catholics were not okay, I was drawn to the Catholic Church. When I was eight and there was a Catholic church between the Protestant Sunday school and my great aunt's house, I would sneak into the church on my way home. Rainbows of light filtering through stained-glass windows and colorfully painted golden statuary thrilled me; but it was a sense of the numinous that kept me coming back, or was it memories from a past life?

March 1978

I record what is received whether or not I understand it or agree with it. If esoteric information is meant to be hidden from the masses, why is it also hidden from those receiving it?

During an initiation, I was encased in a crystal casket and then catapulted into indigo space to be electrified or magnetized.

Chapter Nine
Master Ramana Maharshi

March 23, 1978—Full Moon of Aires

Curious to see what would happen, I attended a two-day class for advanced meditators given by Inayat Khan, the Sufi master who entranced me in January. During the class, he gave interminable lectures about meditation, altered states of consciousness, and esotericism. Most of the concepts were novel, especially the one about masters and their disciples. Before I left, I bought Khan's book *Toward the One*.

That evening, while I was skeptically leafing through the book and looking for a master, I was suddenly arrested by a picture of Sri Ramana Maharshi, a man regarded by many as the greatest twentieth-century Hindu sage. I knew nothing about him, and I wasn't drawn to him by any mental process. His loving eyes pierced my heart. My whole body quivered, and I knew without a doubt that he was my master. After I tore his picture from the book, I framed it and placed it on my dresser.

Before we go any further, I need to remind you that all of the references and quotations following a mystical, extrasensory, paranormal, or transcendent experience were found days, months, or even years after a specific incident.

> In the Hindu traditions, students often perceive their
> gurus to be communicating with them directly, even
> when the student is not in the guru's presence.[1]

Each morning, the palpable love emanating from my master's eyes fills my heart with unconditional love ready for gifting.

In an article, K. G. Durckheim calls for an awareness of the numinous things that happen to awaken us.

> Fleeting contacts with Being, mighty experiences that
> shock us into consciousness and tell us that the time
> has come to change our lives completely. This is when
> we need a master.[2]

This evening, the master directed me to go to my library shelves and pull out any book. Without looking, I chose *The Collected Works of Ramana Maharshi*. Absolutely stupefied, I had no memory of ever buying that book, and as I considered the mysterious things that were happening to me, perhaps it had just been manifested by the master himself. As I stood there and looked at his picture on the cover of the book, my body began a paroxysm of tremors. After I carefully made my way back to bed, I sat for some time and stared at his face until I fell asleep. That night, we met in a dream. I wondered why he kept one arm away from me. Years later, I read that he died of a sarcoma (malignant tumor) on his left arm.

Staring into my master's eyes made me radiant. My body glowed and trembled as I was lifted up and mysteriously transformed as he claimed me. It was totally incomprehensible.

Tonight, once again as I looked at his picture, a quaking began, and I asked, "Who are you?" To my surprise, he answered the following:

> *Don't you realize we are all One? Shall one*
> *cell in a body be praised more than another?*

But he never told me his name.

Eliade Mircea writes that there are certain individuals who undergo initiations and "become **protégés of the Supernatural Beings**."[3]

Because he knew about the trouble occurring in a meditation group

I was conducting, the master spoke the following words:

> *Dear woman, think not on these disturbances, your work is to guide the group with love and wisdom. Always remember that we are one. You have been raised up. Maintain that consciousness.*

Burdened with preparing lectures for my group, teaching, household and other responsibilities, I was depleted.

This morning, when I greeted the master, he told me to light a candle. Brazenly, I responded, "I never light candles," but he insisted, "*Stare at the flame!*" After I stared at the flame for a while, I quit, because nothing seemed to be happening. Despite my brashness, the master used the flame to gift me with a profusion of energy. Day and night for the next three months, I was able to do the work of at least three people.

Robert Adams' earliest memories were of a "two-foot-tall, white-bearded man standing at the end of his crib who would talk gibberish to him." Years later, Yogananda sent Adams to India to find his guru. He found the man who spoke an incomprehensible language to him when he was a small child. The man who became his guru was my master, Ramana Maharshi.[4]

Knowing that Ramana Maharshi had appeared to someone else would have helped me believe in the reality of my encounters with him.

June 1978

Since May, I have been experiencing extreme changes in blood pressure and other symptoms that have resulted in visits to the ER. Today, I asked for help in learning to control the electrical currents that are causing my physical and emotional instability. I was told to visualize the figure eight and to stabilize at the points of intersection, I did so, and it helped.

August 1978

In a dream, the pope told me that I was to be ordained. The next morning as I was still dreaming, bishops and other high-ranking church officials in attendance, I was called forward, dressed in a scarlet robe, and told that I was the only woman who had achieved that position in the church. Tears of joy and humility flowed freely. Was this a dream or a memory? Much later, I was told by an ascended master that I had been Catherine of Siena, one of only two female saints who had been ordained doctors of the Catholic church.

December 1978

My chakras are being activated, allowing me to see everything in a new way. Colors are iridescent. Sounds are musical. Tastes titillate, and my skin is super sensitive. Everything, animate and inanimate, vibrates with energy that I can feel and sometimes see.

Chapter Ten
Initiations

January 1979

Today, a larger-than-life amorphous entity approached me, warning, "*Remain still.*" My head was squeezed into an elongated triangular shape. Given a sword to hold, I was encased in a crystalline coffin that then blasted off like a rocket. An hour later, back in my body and unable to remember anything after the blastoff, I was told not to share this experience with anyone. I have kept it secret until now.

The full moon of Capricorn is having a powerful impact. At 6:00 AM, once again stretched into a rocket shape, I blasted off. The trip was rough but peaceful. When I found myself in an ashram, I asked, "What is the plan?"

A strange master answered, *That all men realize that they are one.* Then he shocked me three times with an electrifying rod. Back in my physical body, I knew that the master and the ashram were now accessible to me. This was not a dream; it seemed to be the second part of the initiation I was told not to talk about.

After several days of resisting the direction to read, the pressure became irresistible at five o'clock one morning. I scanned the bookshelves beside my bed, pulled out *The Spirit of the Upanishads,* but put it back. As I reached for another book, one of the brackets supporting the shelf shot out of the wall, leaving the other one holding the shelf and some of the books in place. I was able to reinsert the bracket to keep the shelf and the rest of the books from falling, but one of my sculptures, a monkish figure, fell, shattering its head as it struck, breaking the glass top of the dresser. The intact body tumbled to the floor with some books. Because of the suddenness and strangeness of the incident, I carefully noted everything. Three books fell, face up: *The Spirit of the Upanishads, Looking Glass God,* and *The God Within*. In an attempt to make sense out of what had happened, I picked up *The Spirit of the Upanishads*, and I read the following:

> How can books enlighten that lump of clay fashioned
> in the form of man, who does not in any manner
> realize the Truth explained to him with all possible
> clearness.[1]

While I stood pondering the meaning of the disparaging message, something ominous entered the room with a blast of arctic air, even though the door and the windows were closed. Frightened by the whole bizarre episode, I left the room. The next morning, still abashed and confused by the strange synchronicity of last night's events, I cleaned up the mess—broken glass, ceramics, and scattered books. Because this had happened after an extended initiation and it had been powerfully negative, I wondered if the intent was to scare me and somehow block my spiritual evolution.

There was a beam of light coming from my eyes and falling on things that were to my left. When I focused on an illuminated spot, it vanished. When I stopped focusing, the golden light returned.

The name "Caleb" entered my mind. Later, I read that he was one of the men allowed to enter the "promised land."

Another powerful negative energy was pervading everything, and my cleansing rituals were unable to remove it.

When I read that mystics "easily succumb to respiratory diseases, digestive problems, and circulatory problems,"[2] I wondered why.

At that time, I had all but circulatory problems.

February 1979

I was being reprimanded in the following message:

You are scattering precious energies on trivia while you should be focusing on the transformation of your brothers and sisters by loving them. Can you be trusted to use the powers for the fulfillment of the plan?

I became aware of a new sense of purpose directing me, and I heard:

Follow the soul, not the ego. We only have the power that you allow. The initiate is never coerced. She must cooperate consciously. Remember renunciation, assembly, celebration, the master, the directing, the trust, and the work. Love raises vibration.

The Master is sent…to the earth by the spiritual hierarchy for a spiritual mission … he could select (and train) those whom he desires to help him.[3]

March 1979

A strong vibration, accompanied by a strange word, "hierophant," awakened me. The dictionary meaning is the following: "a priest who resides over sacred mysteries." *Initiation, Human and Solar* says that the hierophant is one who officiates at the third initiation.[4]

Is that what I had experienced in January?

While I was meditating, I found myself headed toward a light at the end of a dark tunnel. Although I didn't see any figures, the Christ predicted the following:

The path which you must travel to reach your

home is one of light—its quality is goodwill and it is almost ready for your feet. Failure is not for you.

Christ entered my body in 1973. He also entered my life from time to time as a felt-presence, but this was the first time he delivered a message.

How totally ineffable my life is. I keep asking, "Why me?"

> **Grace falls like rain on** everyone but, also like rain, it can only be received by a vessel properly prepared to catch it. [The preparation is], spiritual discipline and self-purification.[5]

April 1979

As soon as a golden light highlighted the words on the page, I was out of my body, hurtling through indigo space filled with a gyrating web pinpointed by multicolored gems. Space is not empty but filled with vibrant life. The physical body contains vortices of energy. As I opened my eyes and expected to be out in space, I was back in my body but still able to see the jeweled web.

When he speaks of "cosmodrama," Deepa Kodikal says, *"I was at a point beyond the earth watching this busy, hurling universe…beyond the endless complex of galaxies."*[6]

During meditation, seven symbols were brought before me in the below sequence. (See Figure 1)

1. A light blue triangle in the center of a golden circle.

2. An indigo square divided into four parts by an X.

3. A shimmering six-pointed star.

4. A flaming, upright violet cross.

5. A sparkling clear triangle with the apex pointing downward.

6. Seven Hebrew letters "HE," like thresholds getting smaller and smaller as they receded in perspective.

7. A crown emitting a spectrum of flaming colors from red to violet.

As the symbols dissolved, I floated on a violet cloud and was raised on shafts of light that penetrated a crystal ball in the heart of a jewel. Every cell in my body was jubilantly ecstatic as I was gently brought back into the physical body on a thread of light. Although my symbols do not resemble the pictures of chakras, they do correspond to them. The Hebrew letter "HE" occurs twice in the name of Jehova, God.

The immanent God (point) within Soul (triangle) is surrounded by its macrocosmic primordial home (circle).

As one falls into physical being, the individual now has the choice of moving in the two possible directions indicated by the apexes.

The choice is made. The soul awakens. Light comes into one's life, and the darkness of the square is escaped.

The individual is determined to let the dross be burnt. He mounts the burning cross, which is symbolic of the suffering one endures on earth.

Once on the path, help from above enters.

Thresholds loom. Gates open to other worlds.

Finally, he assumes mastery of himself (the limited human), and he radiates light and love, becoming one with life, now ready for return.

Figure 1

Manly Hall said:

Symbolism is the language of mystical experience.[7]

Two days after the symbols appeared, *"You exist only by my will,"* thundered forth, causing a trembling throughout my body.

Today I received this poem:

Why are we body-bound
While in unbounded life?
Fields of energy,
Clinging to the body
While the soul is free.

May 1979

The first two weeks of this month, the fifty-third year of my life, brought another dark night of the soul. I thought, "Christ did not take Himself off the cross. Socrates did not leave the country but drank the hemlock. Learn to bear the cross and drink the poison. Do not let the circumstances of your life scar you."

> *When you reside in the consciousness of the world, you are in hell. Rise above this veil of tears while your body bears the scars and tastes the poison. You are of no use to your brothers when you sink so low. Learn from this so that you may be of better service to the hierarchy. You are needed as a channel. Do not sully the vessel. Remember who you are. Stop worrying about where you are. It matters not where you are or what you are experiencing. What matters is who you really are. You cannot be reached*

when you think. Your place is with us on high—a place of light, peace, love, and ecstasy. The door has been opened. Remain with us. This is your home. When you allow your vibration to be lowered, you are of no use to your ascended brothers.

We exist in another dimension and at a different vibratory rate. If you keep us in mind, you will remain in light, peace, and love. The door is wide open for you to come and go at will. This is your true home. This is your Father's house. The table is set. The feast is prepared, and yet you do not join us. You choose to remain in the hell that you have created.

Your masters love you and are aware of your difficulties. Abide with us in faith, hope, and love as earth becomes more hellish day by day. You will join us one day, but until then, shed light and love, which is greatly needed.

As I record these words, I recognize how inscrutable they are.

May 1979

Another poem was transmitted:

Strange life
Living, soul-infused
In worldly cacophony,
Unable to hear the master's call,
trying to balance matter and Spirit.

June 1979

The energy in my meditation group is no longer cohesive. One by one, members are dropping out, and I am almost the last to recognize the problem.

July 1979

After more than a month, the darkness has lifted. Negativity dismembered the group. This experience taught me to be more sensitive to negative energy as I have been challenged to do by my masters.

While I was attempting to contact the master's ashram, my body began to shake, and I spiraled upward until a powerful force stopped me. Back in my body, I was cured of the stress and negativity of the last several weeks, and the pain in my back was gone.

With the command *"Let the child go,"* I saw two children crossing an open field, a girl who was about eleven years old (me) and her little brother, who was about five (my husband). The boy ran ahead and fell into a pit or a well. His sister felt responsible for his death. Was this vision demonstrating the order, "Let the child go," telling me to leave my husband or let him be? I determined that it more than likely meant the latter. His clinical depression was tangible. At its worst, the moment he entered a room, I got a chill, and occasionally, my body even went numb. Despite the difficulty and pain of living with a chronically depressed person, I chose to stay, because I loved him. He needed me, and I had a karmic debt to pay.

The moment I wondered how it would feel to be as depressed as he was, I found myself falling into a dark, bottomless pit. I quickly ended the intention.

That evening, while I read by lamplight, the room filled with golden light. I stopped and waited for a message. I heard, *"Words are not necessary for communication. Symbols suffice."*

> I noticed that the candle was about to go out ... the
> **light** continued ... I saw that it **issued from me**.[8]

August 1979

For two days, I have been drifting in and out of meditation. Tonight as I watched TV, part of me went elsewhere while my senses were fully aware of what was happening on the television. I was in two different places at the same time.

Two days ago, an influx of energy almost sent me out of my body. I mused, "We are spiritual beings, existing in another dimension, projecting a small center of consciousness into a physical body in order to experience life on this planet. The purpose is personal and planetary evolution." I caught glimpses of my other potential selves living in different dimensions of time and space. Everything was really happening now. As visions and insights continued to come, I then knew that evil existed only as a transitory human experience.

> In a state of Essence, all-knowing is direct knowing,
> which goes beyond space, time and personality; all
> senses and all systems are, "go."[9]

> In Essence we find ourselves hooked into perceptions
> and capacities that seem far beyond our own, and
> we gain access to knowing that transcends our given
> experience.[10]

October 1979

Since this morning, I have been in a continuous meditative state. A sense of previous or concurrent lives is submerging the present incarnation. The insignificance of the present life saddens me. The body and mind imprison me in a manifestation from which I wish to escape. The purity and devotion of a spiritual life once lived calls again. From whence have I come this distance? And for what purpose? I am a fragment of my true self, a projected image, a figment of my mind's creation. The real me is experiencing multiple universes and multiple realities.

In my mind's eye I saw a T, a Y, and an X which strangely seemed to represent multiple realities I have been sensing.

November 1979

While I was reading the last few chapters of *Man is Not Alone* by Heschel, I began to weep and then sob. For almost an hour, I wept and shook. Why? I identified with the yearning for spiritual living and piety. I vowed to renounce all and dedicate myself to serving God. I sent love to everyone I knew. Where were these feelings coming from? Could they have been from previous or concurrent lives?

> We are not limited by the laws of biology as we know them today.[11]

Chapter Eleven
Healings

January 1980

Since December, I have had many levitation and flying dreams and out-of-body excursions while fully awake. Angelic images flit in an out of my peripheral vision. Several acquaintances have told me that I have visited and blessed them in dreams.

My voices said to put a note on the school bulletin board offering to teach meditation. I refused, explaining that this could become a problem, but the command continued. Eventually, I posted a notice. Almost immediately, people began to sign up.

The first group I led was for the parents of children in my class. Although the chairs in my classroom were arranged in a circle, my teaching assistant sat on the floor in a yoga position. The next parent to enter, noticing my assistant on the floor, tried to assume the same position, though she was in near-term pregnancy. When I grabbed her arms to seat her in a chair, she became entranced. With a full complement of parents, the meditation proceeded. At the conclusion of the session, the pregnant woman, now out of a fifteen-minute trance, stretched, rubbed the back of her neck, and gasped.

"What's wrong?" I asked.

She joyfully responded, "The tumor on the back of my neck is gone." I hadn't known about the tumor before.

Mrs. L, another parent was scheduled for medical tests to determine the cause of several very serious symptoms: lapses of memory, blackouts, and momentary blindness.

We were about to begin our meditation when I was telepathically directed to put my head beside hers. With her permission, I did so. This was most unusual, because I had never been directed to touch or even approach anyone before.

Some time later, one of the parents told me that Mrs. L had enrolled her children in Catholic school. During the next few months, I would occasionally see her passing by the school. One day, I called to her and asked about her health. After she paused for a moment or two, as if she didn't remember her physical problems, she told me that she was well and that because she had not experienced more symptoms, she had never gone back to the hospital for more tests. I silently praised God.

The first time I used my hands to heal, the heat transferred to the patient, and her pain left almost immediately.

March 1980

In a dream, my husband, who was near death after an automobile accident, was being moved along the corridor of a hospital on a gurney. Terrified, I pleaded with God not to take him and offered the dog I was carrying as a substitute.

That morning, I begged my husband not to go to work, but he went anyway. Several months later, his car was hit and turned upside down. Fortunately, his seatbelt had saved him, or had it been my pleading and offering during the dream?

Without knowing why, I formed a heart with my hands, visualized them holding a sword upright, and sang, "There is no light but Thine. There is no will but Thine. There is no life but Thine." Instantly, full of bliss, I found myself in a realm of light and love.

One has to ride out the turbulence of life as one would ride the waves in the ocean. One must be resurrected after crucifixion for cosmic suffering. Where these thoughts come from I don't know, but I do know that they are not mine and that they are different from what I call the messages and voices.

Chapter Twelve
Symbols

For many, the most profound guidance ... seems to speak the language of symbol and metaphor.[1]

April 1980

In 1978, the inner music of the spheres began, elevating me in body and spirit. It has returned.

During meditation, I saw the equation $2x3R^2=\sqrt{27}$ or 21. It arrived with the words "subatomic particles." For years, I have been working to unearth its meaning. According to numerology, R, the first letter of my name, equals nine, the number of the goddess, according to Joseph Campbell. He elaborates on the significance of nine in many cultures and throughout time.[2]

Three times R (3x9) equals twenty-seven, raised to the second power equals 729. Eighteen times two equals thirty-six, and three plus six equals nine. If the numbers in the square root of twenty-seven (5.19615242271) are added, they also equal nine. I read that three, nine, and twenty-seven are mystical numbers.

> 72, one of the most sacred numbers in the Old Testament of the Jews and in their Qabbalistic system.[3]

Immediately following the equation, I received a chemical formula AL(OH)3. I never studied chemistry, and I was never good in math. If you turn the three over, it becomes "m," and you have Alohem. Elohem is one name of God. When I searched through my husband's college chemistry books, I discovered to my amazement that AL(OH)3 is the formula for aluminum hydroxide, the only truly balanced substance, one equally acid and alkaline. Is this another message about balance? All the numbers in that chemical analysis also seemed to add up to the number nine.

In October 2009, while I was rereading my bibliographic notes, I discovered that Manly P. Hall claimed that both "al" and "el" refer to God. That cleared up the confusion I had about the difference between "Alohem" and "Elohem,"[4] but it did not clarify my confusion about the meaning of the equation or the formula.

Symbols are often used because they contain many levels of meaning.

Symbols are vehicles for inner transformation.[5]

A symbol can never be fully interpreted. It can only be experienced.[6]

The content of a symbol is not irrational, but supra-rational, that is to say purely spiritual.[7]

When I heard, *"All life is spirit, and spirit is a manifestation of God,"* a silver thread connected to a heart pulled me up as a spider raises its prey for the next meal. When I looked down, I saw everything on this planet being fed into one end of a huge wood chopper and being spit out of the other end as new life forms. Is life on this planet in need of total transformation? Now I can say it is, with certainty.

As a brilliant light warmed my body, my head became a large, open lotus blossom that enclosed me in its cool petals, and two vertical parallel lines or thin tubes filled me with a profound peace that lasted for several hours. When I asked for a message I was told, *"I communicate with symbols, not words."*

This morning, an ethereal melody sang of love, joy and the glory of a life filled with gratitude. So transfixed, I could not move to record it.

Numinous dimensions frequently seem more real than the space my physical body occupies. While I am going about my daily activities, my brainwave sometimes switches from beta to theta and then to delta, and I fall asleep. However, occasionally, with some effort, I can remain awake.

Psychologist John Curtis Gowan suggests the following:

> The numinous is like a genie in a bottle that needs release by the conscious personal mind in order to assume its full and powerful service. For short periods of time **the numinous gives the individual access to the whole of human knowledge and experience.**[8]

He equates the experience with tapping into Jung's collective unconscious; however, others disagree. They say that these experiences have nothing to do with tapping into the cumulative thought forms of humanity. I agree with them.

Because of a weekend skating accident, my teaching assistant arrived on Monday with her arm in a cast supported by a sling. An appointment with an orthopedist was made; however, because her husband was unable to take her to see the specialist, I took her instead. The X-rays she carried into the examining room showed two fractures, but the X-rays she carried out showed no fractures, only perfect bones.

In response to a complaint of sleeplessness and fear by one of the members of my parent group, I gently touched her neck and shoulders. That night, she dreamt that her soul descended upon her and removed her fears. She claimed to be free of fear and sleeping well.

A teacher who was not a member of my meditation group told me that she hadn't had a good night's sleep in many years because of tinnitus. I sat with her and meditated. That night, she slept well for the first time in years, and she continued to sleep well after that.

Before class, a teacher came to my classroom wearing chest bindings. Her boyfriend had accidentally broken one of her ribs while giving her a bear hug. During our meditation, I was given the image of her fracture, which I mentally sealed with the Elmer's glue that was sitting on my desk. The next morning, she came to tell me that she was healed. To confirm my vision, I asked her where the break was. It was exactly where I had applied the glue.

Although I never mentioned the healings to anyone, news spread, and teachers, aides, and parents started coming to my classroom for healings. I was also healed of cuts, burns, and sometimes even an ugly wart or two disappeared. However, I took no personal credit for any of the healings.

When I learned that one of the teachers had mouth cancer, I suggested she join us for meditation. She declined. I offered to give her private sessions, but she was still not interested. Many months later, after all conventional medical treatments had failed, I went to her home several times a week at her request to see if I could help. We visualized, meditated, and prayed. After each visit, I left with jaw pain and an inscrutable rage that intensified with every visit. Finally, when my jaw hurt for over an hour after I left her, I knew I could not continue. Subsequently, she tried several overseas alternative medical treatments that also failed. She died.

April 1980

The music of the spheres is so uplifting that I have to check to see if gravity is still doing its job.

A profound influx of unconditional love is making it very difficult for me to restrain myself from hugging everyone.

Working with groups has increased my creativity and intuition. My sculptures create themselves without interference from thought. When something is misplaced, I just visualize it larger than life, and it shows me its hiding place.

This full moon of Taurus has me bubbling over with so much uncontainable energy that I never feel tired.

May 1980

At noon, high voltage electrical charges surged through my body, almost toppling me. It helped to later read that:

> Mystics will experience "**impacts of current** on the brain."[9]

Another message came accompanied by the fragrance of roses:

> *Resist nothing. In your effort to repress thoughts, you create resistance, and the thoughts persist. Things pass out of mind unless rehearsed. Just watch fleeting thoughts and give them no special attention unless they are from us. Thoughts will come and go quickly unless they are rehearsed. Beauty is natural perfection. Right motivation is the axis on which the soul turns. Soul presence creates beauty and value.*

I had the following dreams:

- Offered the choice of several door prizes, I chose a blue veil, although it seemed to be the least expensive.

- A very old man told me that I was wearing a garment of great age and worth. I looked down to see that I was wearing ordinary clothing.

- I was taught the meaning of many esoteric symbols.

- When I heard, "*Come little brother,*" I was lifted out of my body, placed in front of a priestly figure, and offered a communal wafer, which I accepted.

Today's out-of-body travel was as bumpy as riding in a car with broken springs. As I ignored periodic entreaties from beings asking me to stay with them, I continued on my way. Stopped abruptly by an authoritative voice declaring, "*At this time you are unprepared to go any farther,*" I was back in my body. My negative reaction upon hearing that declaration definitely indicated the need for further growth.

For about a year, the pain of high voltage electrical charges took its toll. Presumably, the masters were transitioning me from mystical (emotional) consciousness to occult (higher mental) consciousness, from a life focused on personal enlightenment and spiritual growth to one focused on service to others.

June 1980

In a determined effort to comprehend what is happening, I continue my studies.

Face to face with a master, being offered flowers by children, I heard, "*Un mil veinte,*" which meant one thousand and twenty in Spanish, and I saw a wheel spinning. Asked to name someone who needs healing, I named a friend who had breast cancer. Then I heard, "*Praise God from whom all blessings flow,*" felt a powerful electrical charge, and saw disparate images: a jewel-centered lotus, a red fox, and a Star of David.

My body was being embraced by a brilliant light, and I heard, "Vector," a complex entity represented by any system of equal and parallel line segments. Perhaps these are the shafts of light that sometimes draw me out of my body.

July 1980

The word "primordial" ushers me into the realm of enlightenment, an amorphous dimension of unity, peace, and love, a small Samadhi.

> Based on the scientific evidence, it is no longer
> possible to avoid the conclusion that our perceived

world of separateness and fragmentation is only superimposed on a more fundamental, seamless web of subatomic activity, a vast realm of unbroken wholeness.[10]

I received the symbol of a heart with this message:

Seek neither health nor wealth. Seek only the inner kingdom. The goal of life is to be united with the Father, to be consciously one with God. You know the way—prayer, contemplation and meditation, the recognition of the Christ, the love of God, and the love of man. Carry this message in your mind where you will always remember the principles, and in your heart. Dwell upon that which has been given to you from the Father, the gift of the realized Presence. Bless it always that it may increase.

During another small Samadhi, my personal identity was lost. I understood that nothing my body did could interfere with the union of everything. I was part of the consciousness of God.

August 1980

Yesterday, while I was browsing in a bookstore, *The Highest Yoga as Lived by Mouni Sadhu* beckoned. As I flipped through the pages and wondered, "Why this book?" I almost dropped it when I came upon a picture of my beloved Master Ramana Maharshi. Needless to say, I bought it. In the book, Mouni Sadhu mentions that the radiance emanating from the saintly sage's eyes had a strange power to awaken love in others. That was exceedingly true for me. My heart filled with love the first time I saw a picture of him.

This evening during meditation, I was pulled out of body, and was transported to a place where a strange language was being spoken. When I returned to the body, I was able to remember some of the words, but I didn't think to record them phonetically.

October 1980

My husband's treadmill tests showed some blockage in a heart artery. That night during meditation, I saw the blockage and removed it. He never had another chest pain, and further tests showed no blockage.

November 1980

I was awakened at 3:00 AM by loving warmth that coddled and gifted me with profound peace, love, and the joy of being alive. My dog, sensing something, jumped on the bed, licked my hands, and immediately became entranced.

December 1980

After a strong vibration alerted me, the following message came to mind:

> *I shall use all of my loving and devoted disciples.*

January 1981

Unlike the dark night of the soul, when one felt deserted by God, this dark night felt as if I was the deserter drifting away from the very ground of my being. To stop the drift and to affirm my faith, I decided on baptism. Nothing happened while I was in the water, but an opalescent body emerged, a body that turned out to be mine. Following instructions, I stood with my arms and legs angled away from the body to form the shape of a five-pointed star. The star body shattered, spiraled upward as my body lost its solidity, and slumped to the floor. From the depths of despair, a born-again, a former doubting Thomas, joyously arose.

Sharp penetrating shocks to my head caused a two-week-long headache. Besides the fact that I had to endure the weakness and pain of humanity, I had the additional stress and pain of a mystic. How lucky can I be?

Feeling unloved and sorry for myself, I heard the following:

> *The love you seek is the only reality, but you will not find it where you are looking— it is in the heart. I wish to bring about the reestablishment of the unity of life and negate the idea of separateness. Remember, I was the one who told you that we are one (Ramana. Maharshi.) Seek only the real, and one day, others will be brought to that realization. Those who separate themselves are trying to preserve the ego, because they are unaware of the true self. The Piscean Age required separation and ego development; the Aquarian Age requires synthesis and the realization of oneness. The loss of one's ego is the crucifixion, the death of all we mistakenly call real. What lies beyond crucifixion is rebirth, the birth of the soul-infused spiritual being.*

The joyful tears I shed upon hearing this did not wash away my headache.

I often shed tears of joy and gratitude. It hasn't been a serious problem for me, but I do hope it is a tormenting problem for the dark forces that attempt to prevent the spiritual evolution of mystics like me. The following quote may clarify this comment.

> The "charism of tears" displayed by medieval mystic
> Margery Kempe of Lynn, who wept so noisily that
> one of the priests had her kept out of the church
> during services. She consulted Julian of Norwich who
> told her that the **"gift of tears"** according to Saint
> Gerome **"torment more the devil than do the pains
> of hell."**[11]

February 1981

Burning sensations accompanied by excessive nervousness must be
the result of these electrical shocks, because my daily life is moving
along smoothly at this time.

> Eliade Mircea writes that the rising Kundalini is
> manifested by **burning sensations**.[12]

Chapter Thirteen
Transition

March 1981

I know that angels are a different species, so how is it that from time to time I feel as if wings are growing out of my shoulder blades?

After I listened to a lecture on angels at a small church, I approached the minister. Not waiting for me to speak, she just stared at me and whispered something that bewildered and frightened me. "You come from a different stream of humanity." Unable to respond, I walked back to my seat in a puzzled daze, gathered my things, and left.

I forgot about that incident until I started rereading my journals. Today, I addressed my masters and asked them what that minister saw. They answered with the following:

> *What she saw confounded her because it was truly a new form. She saw a human being in transition, a prototype of the new spiritual being who will some day inhabit this planet, one who will use the physical body whenever she deems it necessary, but she will not be burdened by having to stay confined in that body. She will truly have free will.*

March 1981

On *Authority Quotes'* website, I found this quote by J.J. Dewey.

The power of initiation brings the power of joy in service.

Heat and energy moved up and down my body, creating tremors. Then, I floated above my body for several minutes.

Sudden **changes in body temperature, pulse and tremors** are the result of **fiery manifestations**[1]

April 1981

Vibrations are becoming more intense and more frequent, as is the feeling of being overtaken by something transcendent. Despite this, or perhaps because of this, I am filled with joy and peace. The glow coming from my body illuminates the page as I write. The music of the spheres plays, and I see violin strings being tightened. Am I the strings or the violin? When you give yourself to God, He can do whatever He wants to do with you, even tighten your strings to raise your vibration.

May 1981—Full Moon of Taurus

The music penetrates, creating harmony throughout my body. In a dream, I was seated at a round table with other accepted disciples. *"Do you know what it means to be an accepted disciple?"* I was asked. Before I could reply, my aunt, who died early this year, took me into another room and proceeded to answer all of my unvoiced questions. As usual, I do not remember the questions or the answers.

The master was telling me that stronger vibrations would be used to change my consciousness. Immediately, several electrical shocks stiffened my body, and the top of my head opened.

The **master** begins to **test** him out by the application of some **higher vibration** and by the study of his reaction to that vibration.²

July 1981

This month I experienced the past-life regressions that follow:

In Caracas, Venezuela a wizened, toothless, one-eyed curandero (healer) wearing sandals and a long, coarse robe is leaning on a staff while gathering medicinal herbs. Many people are waiting outside his cottage to be healed. The regression ended, and the eye, which was missing in that former life, hurt and began to tear now.

My daughter asked me to regress myself in an attempt to understand why she felt such unprovoked anger toward me. Although all of my previous regressions had been spontaneous, I was willing to try.

We sat on the bed opposite one another, and when I took her hands, she became a man. My neck muscles tightened, and I was aware of a swarthy, shabbily dressed man behind me.

It was evening in the late nineteenth century, and a stylishly dressed woman seated in a nicely decorated parlor was reading a book. I, the observer, could see the room in great detail. The woman, unaware of the swarthy intruder's presence, continued reading until she felt his hands around her throat.

Trying but unable to stop the regression, I drifted further back in time and found myself hanging from chains in a large stone torture chamber. Through a small opening in the heavy wooden door, I saw the demonic face of an ugly man highlighted by flickering light, gleefully leering at me. My captor entered the room, picked up an ax, and with one blow, hacked off my right arm. While still in the regression, I felt my right arm become numb and then disappear altogether. My daughter's pleading, "Mom, what's happening?" finally broke the regressions and brought me back. Before I could speak, I looked for my right arm, which I could not feel. After several more requests by my daughter, I relented and revealed what had happened. Though I expected her to be as shaken and appalled as I was, she showed no distress. Equally unexpected and shocking was what she told me. When, as a child, it was her turn to share with playmates her idea of a perfect bedroom, she described a room with stone walls. She did not reveal her torture fantasies, which surely would have left her without friends.

The next day, we visited her therapist, whose reaction to our story was surprising. The therapist said, "You and your mother incarnated together once again so that you could make amends for having killed her in at least two previous lives." The therapist and my daughter validated the regression episodes.

Back home in California, two more incarnations were spontaneously unveiled. Seated in a sparsely but exquisitely furnished spacious room overlooking a manicured garden, a wealthy and powerful white-bearded Chinese man dressed in an elaborately embroidered silk gown sat. In another incarnation, a Japanese samurai sat on a floor mat in a very small room. (I wish I could remember what I was supposed to learn from my past lives.)

Despite the fact that I had the loving attention of the masters, my physical problems continued.

August 1981

There was a palpable negativity and heaviness in the house, so I sprinkled salt on the windowsills of the open windows, burned incense, and blessed the rooms by making the "sign of the cross" in each doorway. I didn't know whether these things were working or not, but I did them anyway.

October 1981

The woman who introduced me to meditation in 1968, now my friend, invited me to become the third member of a meditation/study group. I accepted.

December 1981

It has been many years since Christ entered my body and consummated our mystical marriage, but this evening, His presence made me painfully aware of my failings. I rededicated myself to a life of service.

An angel with luminous white wings appeared before me. Perhaps they were not wings but energy fields. She prophesied, "*You too shall mount on wings as angels do.*"

January 1982

During one of the new meditation group meetings, it was my turn to read. In the middle of a sentence, I was unable to continue. My heart was beating rapidly, my breathing shallow, and waking consciousness was slipping away. As I lay on the daybed in another room, I saw a sword being forged in a fire and a group of masters evaluating me from above. I was lifted and wrapped in a cocoon of opalescent light, but my rapture abruptly ended when I was told by my friend that it was time to go home. Since then, everything is scintillating energy, and everyday reality blinks on and off.

Tonight, during group meditation, my body was consumed by a purple flame that burned its way through my solar plexus, heart, throat, and eyes. It then exploded through the top of my head like a volcano.

During our habit of farewell embracing, my excessive body heat was noticed by the others.

Another poem:

We create a world of images
While the still-small voice of reality whispers,
"Here I am!"

Because I never felt that this meditation group was right for me, I withdrew. My friend graciously accepted my resignation and took me to meet the leader of another group. The moment I met her, my heart opened, and love showered out. For quite a while, this loving feeling for a stranger was a mystery.

February 1982

The masters reported:

There is only one way, the lighted way, and each of us must find it for him or herself. It is the way of the heart. There is no darkness in reality. There is only the absence of light and love.

March 1982

Another transmission:

You are being trained to channel healing love. Become pure physically, mentally, and emotionally, and you will be of greater use to us. You have been chosen to be guided. Avoid anything that will contaminate. God is expressing Himself through each of us according to our readiness and willingness to think and act rightly.

Study "A Course in Miracles." (A book that was transmitted to Dr. Helen Schuman.) *You must learn self-mastery. Free yourself from your social conditioning. Self-mastery begins with vigilant self-observation and a willingness to change. Once you commit yourself to this purpose, you will be assisted by us. As you know, your training is being telepathically communicated. You are responsible for the self-mastery. A true healer is one who has total mastery of the lower self. Your training did not begin with my entry into your life. It commenced at birth, but the decision was made before that. Time is of the essence. Do not waste it. Cut away that which is not purposeful. Align your will with the will of God. Every cell in your body becomes more conscious as you become more conscious. You can control and maintain your body's health and youthful vigor if you take control of your thoughts and actions.*

Every crisis is an opportunity. Eternal life is already yours. You will achieve your soul's purpose for this incarnation. There is no need to go looking outside for anything. Everything you need is already yours.

Telepathy and clairvoyance depend on the thickness or thinness of the threshold between the self-conscious and the subconscious mind.[3]

Chapter Fourteen
Experiences Continue

May 1982

At 3:33 in the morning, awakened by a strong impulse to teach and serve, I heard, "*I told you that you would be picking the lilies of the fields.*" (Lilies must represent people, because I'm now working with groups.)

During my morning meditation, I heard, "*Adi, heart of the sun, rainbow-bridge, and light at the end of the path.*" In *Treatise on Cosmic Fire*, "Adi" is the plane of divine manifestation, the first plane of our solar system. Heart of the sun is the place where the great "rod of power" of the Logos Himself is hidden. The rainbow bridge is the antakarana, the path between the personal and the impersonal self.[1]

All of this means little to me at this time of my life. Perhaps I will understand it someday.

My meditation was so deep that I became totally unaware of the other members of the group. Several geometric figures flashed by flooding me with the heat of kundalini as it passed through the chakras and erupted out of the top of my head.

This morning, a message came telling me that a breakfast of dried fruit would be what I needed to cure my sore throat. I had thought that a salt-water gargle would be prescribed, but the fruit devas did their job.

Since Thursday, the weakening of my ego is making it difficult to perform ordinary tasks.

June 1982

Knocked out of my body by what felt like a lightening strike, I left my body. I experienced what is described below by Gopi Krishna.

> Suddenly ... I felt a mood of deep absorption
> settling upon me until I almost lost touch with my
> surroundings ... I suddenly felt what seemed to be **a
> mighty conscious presence, sprung from nowhere.**
> Another deep absorption happened ... I had
> expanded in an indescribable manner ... conscious
> from within of an immediate and direct contact
> with an intensely conscious universe, a wonderful
> inexpressible immanence all around me.[2]

Though I only knew that "AUM" was a Hindu mantra, I was fixated on the middle letter, "U," for some strange reason.

Subsequently, I read, "The secret of the fire lies hid in the second letter of AUM."[3] (See glossary.)

I awoke at 2:45 AM with the image of an eight-faceted diamond and heard *"Diamond Sutra."* In *Stalking the Wild Pendulum*, Bentov describes the diamond as the symbol of material life transmuted into spiritual life.[4] Years later, I searched online and read that the "Diamond Sutra" was defined in the following way:

> The perfection of wisdom of the diamond that
> cuts through illusion [and] teaches the wisdom
> of avoidance of abiding in extremes of mental
> attachments.

While I was meditating this evening, I was given a crown, a giant crystal, a rod, and a message about light, love, and power. Puzzled, I once again found myself motivated to seek answers in the world, for that which can only be found within.

Love is the clue to successful telepathic work.[5]

During the full-moon meditation, a vast, dazzling, triangular, multicolored network of diamonds revealed itself. Transfixed by the splendor of the image, I was alerted by a diamond-tipped rod touching my head and lifting me out of my body. As a person is drawn to join a circle of dancers, I floated toward and joined a network of diamond souls. Back in my physical body, I shed tears of joy. During these happenings, my intellect is not functioning, but a knowing beyond the mental is. Occasionally, I am able to think and know alternately during unordinary events.

The rod of initiation is surmounted by a diamond.[6]

Today, during the usual housecleaning, I was arrested by the nonsensory experience of being wrapped in a cocoon of extraordinary beauty, love, and joy while the world about me remained ordinary.

During group meditation, I was overcome by a nonvisual brilliance, my throat chakra began spinning like a top, causing an uncontrollable cough that forced me to leave the group.

This morning, a huge, shimmering, triangular angel filled the room with a love so penetrating that I swooned.

After breakfast, my sense of self dissolved along with an awareness of time and space. Only pure consciousness existed. Like the perforations on a player-piano roll, I saw points of light revealing an indecipherable code. Was this the Akasha, a quantum field of information that I could understand during what I called my Satori?

My perspective was being changed by words and ideas that entered from higher levels of reality. Ordinary objects had taken on a mysterious otherworldly energy that was impossible to explain.

Once again, a flame consumed my gross body. A smokelike plume exited the top of my head, causing profuse perspiring. When the group meditation ended, I checked the cushion. It was very hot, as was my body, for several hours. (This also happened in January.)

I have begun to accept, without too much resistance, these incomprehensible events.

In an effort to discover the inexplicable love I felt for the leader of the new meditation group, I decided to attempt a regression.

The mother superior of a convent was given a baby girl whom the nuns had found abandoned outside the gates. As the child grew, the mother superior (me) became excessively attached to her. Staggered by her beauty, I often secretly watched her dancing with abandon in the courtyard, her golden hair catching the sun as she twirled around.

When she reached maturity, my dream of her becoming a nun was dashed, for she decided to leave. With an aching heart, carefully lifting her spun-glass hair, I placed a cross on a silver chain around her neck and kissed her good-bye. Years later, surrounded by praying nuns, I held on to life with the hope of seeing her before I died, sinfully longing for her rather than for my Lord.

Out of the regression, I snatched my sketch pad in an effort to record the beautiful image of her dancing form as she spun, hair airborne. The love I feel is not for the woman she now is but for the memory of who she once was.

When our meditation group disbanded, my golden girl and I continued our friendship. She moved to Northern California some years ago, and I regretted never having visited her before she died.

In a dream, I was shown that square shapes could only be folded into halves or thirds and that the rest of the folds were multiples of two or three. Four folds equaled six or eight parts. Thirds folded made nine. Two made five. One fold made two parts.. When I woke, I tried to see if this was true, but I soon gave up.

I am being guided to read *Light on the Path* by Mabel Collins and *The Light of the Soul* by Alice Bailey.

July 1982

During our group meditation, we visually created a garden and a sanctuary in which we deposited all of our negativity. That night, in a dream, I recreated the garden. Everything was the same—the orderly rows and circles of flowers, the path, straight and narrow—but the sanctuary was larger and opalescent, a small version of the Taj Mahal. I entered the sanctuary and prostrated myself before the altar. Instantly, I was taken out of my body, and everything became one nonphysical, energy field.

That same evening, as I was driving home before the dream, my headlights would not turn on. I was able to get only a very dim light from the high beams. The next morning, I took the car to the dealership. They kept the car for a day and a half but could find nothing wrong. Was this another message from the masters about light?

While I was reading *The Spiritual Teaching of Ramana Maharshi*, I was amazed at the similarities between what he taught others and what he taught me. (He began my training in 1978, and he died in 1950.) These are some of the similarities:

The unity of all selves.
When I first asked, "Who are you?" his answer was the following: "We are one."

Who am I?
The mantra he recommended for meditation was the theme of the first lecture I gave to a group long before I had found him.

The heart is the seat of the Self.
He taught me how to ascend the silver cord to reach his heart.

Camera metaphor.
He told me that humanity's reality is an image projected onto a screen from a higher reality.

The light is the Self.
He often made me light candles.

It does not help to change the environment.
He told me this many times.

"The Self is the heart, self-luminous. You see the world by the reflected light of the Self."[7]
He used reflections to explain things to me.

Mahadevan wrote that people who knew Master Ramana Maharshi spoke of the blessing of his loving gaze. This was the love I still felt when I looked into his eyes.[8]

While asleep, I was taught the significance of color and sound.

In a self-induced regression, I saw myself and my best friend, an African America woman, as children on a plantation playing a circle game with other black kids. When the scene changed, we were young women hurriedly packing our scanty belongings in blanket rolls. The regression ended with us scurrying through the woods at night.

The next morning, I telepathically received the name Harriet Tubman and the year 1918. After I checked the encyclopedia, I was stupefied to learn that she was one of the conductors of the Underground Railroad. But because Tubman died in 1913, I wondered why I was given the date 1918.

When I was quite young, I remembered wondering why I had been born so pale. I had expected to see a black face when I looked into a mirror.

Although I have been trained by Sri Ramana Maharshi for many months without ever actually seeing him, he appeared to me tonight, hovering above me. As he directed, I tried ascending the silver cord that connected our hearts, but the heat and vibration were too potent for me.

Because my back was aching, he instructed, *"Bring the heat to your back."* As he displayed a string of figure eights leading to his heart, he continued, *"Move up as far as you can and pause at the intersections to stabilize. "Say, Master Ramana, I invoke you for your counsel. Now expand."*

As I followed his instructions, I became crystal clear, not mentally but physically. *"Now, contract and reenter your physical body,"* he said. A penetrating G note returned me to my physical body. This was not a dream. I fully awake during the whole process, and my back no longer ached.

I lit the candle beside my master's picture and asked for a sign that would assure me that I was not hallucinating. Because he did not respond, I started to leave the room, but when I remembered the candle, I returned to extinguish it. The flame bent but did not go out. I blew harder, and the flame bent again. I blew even harder a third time, but it did not go out. I tried a fourth time with the same result. Then the master ordered, *"Now blow it out!"* The flame was extinguished

Many years later in *Treatise on Cosmic Fire*, I read "When the fire descends from the One, the wind suffices not to blow it out."[8]

Yesterday, master's face was a flaming green cross. Today, it is the universe. I see black holes, stars, and planets. The master is the fire. Through his eyes, you enter a black hole and pass into another universe. We all are universes. (I wrote about a black hole before I ever heard of what astrophysicists called a black hole.)

After breakfast, I sensed a presence that said, *"Are you willing to experience a trance?"*

"If I can remember what happens," I answered.

Again, the silver cord leading to my master's heart appeared. As I ascended and used the figure eight as the master had instructed, I was told to visualize myself on top of a mountain and then to raise my arms above my head. I followed directions and found myself looking down on our beautiful, blue planet. As I zoomed in, I saw the United States, California, South Pasadena, my home, my sleeping husband, and my own body sitting in meditation. Before I reentered my body, I was given a bit of the solar angel's consciousness so that I would be able to summon her if necessary. This event took place during a meditative state. I was not asleep, and I had never heard of a solar angel before.

Although at times during meditation I can reach incredibly elevated states in normal consciousness, I am often filled with negativity and anger, mostly toward my husband. I asked the master if we should divorce. The answer was a definite no! *"You have much to learn about yourself from the way you react to this man."*

Tonight, while I was preparing for bed, I had the distinct impression that I was going to die. Without any emotion, I wrote a farewell note and went to sleep. It was morning when a blast from the radio brought me back to life. My body was stiff, cold, and unresponsive. Had I really died?

> When the Shakti (power) has reached the upper
> brain ... the whole body is **cold and corpselike.**[9]

The shimmering, triangular-shaped angel appeared again. Was this the solar angel?

I had another angel experience today. W hile a group from my retirement community was attending a concert in the park, I saw a huge angel-shaped cloud. Because I knew that I often saw things that others did not, I asked the woman beside me what she saw. She replied, "An angel." Later that evening while I was looking up at the sky from my balcony, the very same angel cloud was looking down at me.

August 1982

The master is signaling when he wants me to meditate. Today, after meditation, as I remembered the candle flame that would not extinguish, I blew hard. To my chagrin, the melted wax sprayed the dresser top. When I was about to wipe it up, I was stopped short by the master's face outlined in wax, staring up at me. In disbelief, I asked my husband and later several friends to verify my perception. They also saw a wax image of Ramana Maharshi. How much more proof did I need of my master's reality and power?

> There are as many strata at different levels of life as there are leaves in a book. When on the higher levels we can remember the lower levels, but when on the lower we cannot remember the higher.[10]

This morning I was told the following:

> *Be like a lake of glass, which when a pebble hits, it bounces off unable to act upon the glass surface as it does on water. Your reaction to every ding creates negative karma. You become like whatever you react to. Resistance and judgment create resonance and become your future. Everything is a reflection of your self. Levels of reality are like a movie: there is the subject to be photographed, the perspective of the photographer, the camera, the film, the*

projector, the screen, and the projected image. Which is real? Your physical body is the image projected by your spirit. Many of your little brothers have not even lit a candle and continue in darkness, thinking that they live in light. A master is able to see the light of a flaming heart.

Society has done a very good job of thoroughly indoctrinating me with a materialistic interpretation of reality. I still remain skeptical.

Filled with self-doubt and questioning, I asked for proof. With the patience only possible of an ascended master, Ramana repeated what he had told me many years ago:

We are all one. The very idea of separateness is antithetical to the truth I have been trying to communicate. Light the candle and place it so that the flame is aligned between our eyes. Focus on the flame.

As I stared at the flame, he continued saying:

Stretch your arms out at the level of your shoulders with your palms up. See yourself as a sword surmounted by a diamond. Walk creating these patterns: a circle, a square, a triangle, a cross, and a six-pointed star.

I followed his instructions in a somnambulistic state. He then ordered the following:

Hold your mind steady in the light and keep a point of receptive tension, expecting nothing. It is a lesson in patience and mind control.

Told that I was being trained for the army of Christ, I was charged to learn the esoteric significance of color, sound, and vibration. Was this meant to allay my doubt or to increase it?

When I look back, I wonder how the master was able to continue my training despite my thick-headed inability to trust. I also now recognize that the patterns he had me walk included some of the same figures that I had received on April 26, 1979.

> The conviction of being completely separate individuals makes any conscious communication between two levels impossible.[11]

August 1982

During a morning meditation, I heard the musical note that my master sometimes used to get my attention. He claimed the following:

> *Your training for now is in the proper use of the mind. Use your mind to become receptive to the higher creative planes, imaginative and contemplative. Do not make any personal decisions at this time. The vehicles are being used to enable you to more accurately receive telepathic communications.*

As Aurobindo indicates, one cannot reach what he calls Supermind without help.

> The transition to Supermind through overmind is a passage from Nature as we know it into Super-Nature. It is by that very fact impossible for any effort of the mere mind to achieve; our unaided personal aspiration

and endeavor cannot reach it.[12]

At 11:50 AM, I saw a cross on the top of a mountain, and water was tumbling over the rocks, being purified by the sun.

With the musical note la (A), a very strong current of energy penetrated the top of my head and moved down through my body, whirling each chakra. The experience was aborted when my husband entered the room.

This evening, after I had heard the master's note and felt his vibration, I was told to go into the swimming pool. While in the water, I became painfully aware of my limitations and how much they impeded my usefulness. While I was floating in the pool, I saw the letter "H" imbedded in color-changing backgrounds. Was this Koot Hoomi, who later taught me the significance of color and sound? Master Ramana explained:

> *Because you no longer have an astral body, I use a body of water. Criticism lowers the vibration of the one who criticizes as well as the recipient of the criticism.*

Feeling unworthy of his grace, I cried and silently pleaded, "I believe. Help my unbelief."

Manly Hall calls mysticism a heart doctrine and describes the mystical life as transcending the boundaries of normal physical life. The mystic "transforms the body into an instrument for the use of soul power."[13]

This morning when I kissed my master's picture, his energy entered my nose and burst forth out of the top of my head, and I received a message:

> *The spiritual triad is the flame linking us. The glass covering my picture reflects the spirit.*

During meditation, I saw a grid with horizontal lines crossing vertical lines.

Immediately after waking, the master called me to a several-hour meditation that continued after I fell asleep. I knew that when a sudden sleepiness overtook me, it was a signal to sit quietly and allow the master to take control.

September 1982

During our weekly group meditation, a series of electrical shocks took me from my physical body to a small community of aspirants awaiting an initiation. They appeared as a cluster of rainbow-colored, five-faceted diamonds. When the meditation group members began to leave the apartment, I reluctantly reentered my body. During the drive home, the tires did not meet the road. The car flew above the freeway, or so it seemed.

October 1982

Yesterday, despondent, I lost interest in everything. Today, interest in life and happiness has returned.

After meditation, I accidentally touched the incense, but it did not burn me.

> The effects of ashramic training ... [are] ... jittery
> feelings, a sense of being in no man's land, **depressed,
> disinterested**, having tension or low energy.[14]

The above quote describes my mood swings, and I cannot attribute it to anything that is happening in my ordinary life.

Last night, a huge golden cross immobilized me as a black body bag was slipped over my head. I offered no resistance as it was being pulled down, enclosing my whole body. I presumed that I was dying. In the morning, horrified to still find myself in that frightful bag, I wiggled and chafed like a snake shedding its skin, in an effort to remove it.. Finally free but still lying in bed, I looked up and saw the bag hovering above my body. As it slowly drifted off, I became boundless and filled with light. I was part of everything, and everything was part of me. When I finally stood up, my feet didn't seem to touch the floor. (It is hard to decide which of my experiences is the most bizarre, but this one comes close.)

At this point, it seems appropriate for me to quote Arthur Schopenhauer:

> All truth passes through three stages: First, it is
> ridiculed; next, it is violently attacked; finally, it is
> held to be self-evident.

March 1983

The master informed me that I was being trained to channel healing energy and that I would learn to heal myself and then others. He added that I was also being prepared for mastery of this life experience but that it would require perfect attention and alignment with his vibration by thinking of him and picturing him as often as possible.

Your mind must be held steady in light and your heart steady in love. Only then can you truly manifest the will of God.

Chapter Fifteen
Other Masters

June 1983

Last month, another master assumed my training in a dream. Today, he made his appearance, not in a dream but in reality, my reality. Mahatma Gandhi needed no introduction. He started abruptly, "*You are being trained to work with color and sound. I put my mark on you when you were in India.*" That stopped me, and I began to comb my memory.

Our tour group was hurriedly leaving a museum when I slipped on rain-soaked marble, fell backward, and hit my head. Although I was able to continue the tour, I didn't feel well, so when we returned to the hotel, my husband called for a doctor. Fortunately, the hotel had a doctor in residence whose diagnosis was a slight concussion. In the morning, I checked for bruises. The image I saw had to be confirmed by my husband. Growing up my back was a well-defined, beautiful, large, yellow and purple four-petal flower blooming at the end of a long undulating stem. Because of its uniqueness and beauty, we considered taking a photograph, but because the picture would have revealed more than the flower, we decided against it. Years later, when I saw a picture of Muladhara (root chakra), I remembered my bruise. That had not been any ordinary bruising. It had been Master Gandhi's work of art, and it definitely woke sleeping Kundalini.

Another message arrived:

Although your training will be mental, the vibration you experience will have a profound effect on the physical vehicle of the human, animal, plant, and even the mineral. Fear not, for I am with you and I will be available whenever you need me.

Most of the visits from Master Gandhi took place while I was getting ready for work, and therefore, they are not consciously remembered. I did not remember the statement: "*You are being trained to work with color and sound,*" so I was confounded that summer by the amount of time I spent addicted to crocheting rainbow colored afghans.

Although Master Gandhi was already training me, I was devastated when Master Ramana told me that he was turning my training over to another master. As I kneeled before his picture, I begged forgiveness for doubting the reality of our relationship. I asked why he had chosen me for this exceptional grace. He replied, "*You are pure of heart, and one day, you will become a master.*" He declared that he had to move on but that I would always have access to his heart. Tearfully, I vowed my love and devotion, thanked him, and promised to do everything in my power to become worthy. (A sense of unworthiness and humility always accompanies the elevation of spirit.)

Ghazali, the eleventh-century Sufi mystic, said, "The first requisite of a mystic [is] … purification of the heart."[1]

> The heart center of the human being is therefore like
> a mirror, which must be pure, so that it may receive
> the light of the divine spirit.[2]

In the *Katha Upanishad* we are given three ways to know God.
1. By the Grace of God.
2. By the Purity of heart.
3. By one-pointed contemplation.[3]

I received another poem:

Saint of Arunachala, Ramana Maharshi
I met you in a book.
I knew you not, but you knew me.
My frozen heart was melted by your gaze.
For years you led me
Through the mysteries of life
I knew not why, nor how,
But followed your directions
And found myself.

Today, Master Ramana Maharshi introduced the new Master as Master K. H. He gave no name, just initials. I was confused, because I was already being trained by someone who looked like, and I presumed was, Mahatma Gandhi.

Master K. H. also spoke to me every morning as I was getting ready for work. His manner was identical to the master I thought was Gandhi, so I decided that they were one and the same. Although Master Ramana did not give me his name, I learned that he was the Master Koot Hoomi.

Later, I was surprised to find Alice Bailey's description of Master Koot Hoomi as tall, thin, and wearing a turban, definitely not a description of Mahatma Gandhi. Subsequently I started searching Web sites and found paintings of Koot Hoomi that agreed with Bailey's description.

July 1983

This morning, Master K. H.'s presence was so powerful that I became dizzy and disoriented. After he expressed his approval of my use of creative energies, he showed me a network of jeweled, colored lights with accompanying musical notes:

- *C (Do) red (will)*
- *D (Re) orange*
- *E (Mi) yellow*

- *F (Fa) green*
- *G (Sol) blue (love/wisdom)*
- *B (La) indigo (synthesis)*
- *A (Ti) violet*

He had me sound out each note while I visualized the color. In answer to my unspoken question about why all of the colors were not given meanings, he told me that the meanings were registering subconsciously.

November 1983

When I was talking aloud to the Master K. H., I revealed, "Sometimes I believe that everything that is happening is a figment of my imagination."

He simply replied, "*Oh, one of little faith.*" Then he sounded a la (A) note, and a powerful force surged through my body, almost knocking me over. (I guessed that was proof of his reality and his power.)

December 1983

The Master R. M. is close. He is responding to my call for renewed faith. This time, he produces a Ti [B] note and gives me the following instructions:

See the lighted way. Synthesize will and love and work with the blended energies to accomplish what needs to be done.

My life is very puzzling: electric shocks, esoteric information, instructions that are relayed both consciously and subconsciously, and many disturbing physical symptoms. I mused, Our minds are incapable of understanding what is not meant to be understood, but what other means do we have of knowing? We are so attached to mentality and the rational that we think it is the only way of knowing, but it isn't. In fact, knowing is not a mental experience at all, nor is it rational. As Thomas Moore says:

> There are places in this world that are neither here nor there, neither up nor down, neither real nor imaginary. These are the in between places difficult to find and even more challenging to sustain. Yet they are the most fruitful places of all.[4]

January 1984

During meditation, my head was ablaze with energizing light.

> Mystical experiences must be immediately experienced to be known, and cannot be attained by the logical methods of Western science, philosophy, and theology or described in any determinate way.[5]

May 1984

During a group meditation, I left my body and found myself in the legendary valley of Shambhala during the Wesak Festival. (See glossary.)

July 1984

Christ's energy exploded out of the top of my head.

September 1984

Once again, I am hearing notes and melodies.

December 1984

The scissor-cut was still bleeding as I wiped it with an alcohol swab. About to apply the Band-Aid, though it was not necessary, the finger was healed.

March 1985

During a violent shaking, I saw the Master K. H. and heard him say, *"At last! Calm yourself, dear girl."* Then he directed me to mentally create a university where both teachers and students would learn how to concentrate, meditate, observe, control emotions, change negative energy to positive energy, and express love. He told me that the curriculum that I had previously begun to write had been inspired by him.

May 1985

When I asked the master why I have been absorbing so much negativity in the form of illness, he confirmed the following:

> *Your purpose, planned before this incarnation, was to be a transformer of negative energy, and you have been doing it your whole life. You are a passive healer, acting to transform all forms of negativity and ignorance into positive wisdom. You are a lightning rod. No need to protect yourself in any way other than by maintaining your spiritual ties to the hierarchy and your masters. We will protect you.*

June 1985

While pale blue entities flew about joyously, a flaming Christ and the hierarchy sent jubilant blessings to earth. My body became synchronized with the pulsation of the universe, and I saw an eight-faceted diamond.

I was looking through travel brochures and trying to decide where to go on our next vacation when I intuitively knew it had to be China. Once the decision had been made, everything fell quickly into place.

The plane was nearing Tokyo on the way to China when I looked up to see an unusual figure gliding down the aisle. He wore a long robe, a long white beard, and a mustache. Because of his unusual appearance, I turned to my husband and whispered, "Can you see him?"

"See who?" he asked.

When I realized that this was another one of my paranormal visions, I directed my attention to the visitor, who was now by my side. He said, "*I am pleased that you followed my prompting and chose to come to China. I was one your spiritual advisors many years ago.*"

Without a pause, he continued. "*You needed to come to China to help us balance Eastern and Western energies. With your newly gained receptivity and sensitivity, you are now ready to be trained in channeling.*"

I protested, "I am not interested in channeling."

"*You will not be channeling entities but love. You are one of the many chosen to be silent transformers.*"

I was surprised when he quoted the Bible: "*Those who wait upon the Lord shall mount up on wings as angels ... shall renew their strength.*"

I thought it would have been more appropriate for him to quote Lao Tsu. The visitor continued: *I think you were right not to follow your own will in making career changes. Teaching is the right career for you.* (I had thought of becoming a counselor.)

I asked for the meaning of the seven symbols that I received many years ago, and he explained them. Because he spoke without stopping, he gave me no time to record what he said.

He taught me how to relieve pain by separating the subtle body from the physical body. He said I would not need medications but would be able to heal myself with color, sound, and love. "*You are being prepared for the fourth initiation, but you may need another incarnation to achieve it.*"

I thought, "Oh, please don't let me come back again as a baby."

He advised, "*Do not be so critical of others who are evolving in their own particular way. You have reached a level of spiritual development that allows you to ask questions and receive answers from us, your masters.*"

Then, as suddenly as he appeared, he disappeared.

On our last day in China, as we walked down the "Road of Animals" lined with larger-than-life stone statues, I was astonished to see two statues that looked like the master who had visited me in the 747. I asked my husband to take a picture of them.

Several years later, I called upon the Chinese Master to thank him for directing me to read the *Signs of Agni Yoga* books and to ask why he had never visited me again. He responded immediately with the following:

> The atmosphere of the planet Earth is so densely polluted in many ways that I would rather not enter it unless absolutely necessary. Thank you for coming to China so that I could be with you in a more comfortable setting.

His response filled me with joy, gratitude, and love. I promised to do my best to help lessen the contamination of our planet.

September 1985

A fiery energy coursing through my body was causing migraines, and nothing seemed to relieve the pain. I received the message: "*You asked for illumination, and you're getting it along with the migraines.*"

December 1985

I am being directed to read certain books, and they always reveal something that needs to be learned or remembered. Sometimes the master comes through saying: "*Another small rending of the veil that obscures reality.*"

Chapter Sixteen
Mystics

January 1986

I have been told by friends who are students of metaphysics that I am a Second Ray person.

> Second Ray persons [are] naturally absorbers and
> magnetically attract all that is in their environment
> that is directed towards them.[1]

Suddenly, the Hebrew letter "HE," my threshold symbol (the sixth of of seven symbols that appeared to me in 1979), is showing me that I am being challenged by the guardians of the threshold who question my readiness for the next phase of spiritual evolution. They may also represent my fears.

The desire for perfection is a primary requisite for grace. While I was experiencing one of my many dark nights of the soul, I asked, "Why me? What have I done to deserve God's grace?"

The answer was the same as before: "*You are pure of heart.*"

I had no idea what that meant; however, I do know that I always desired purity.

The following describes me:

The mystic sense of life and adventure of mind strains
upward, beyond all present maps. The world of
the senses of material facts and goals of life is never
enough for him. [2]

In out-of-body travel, I have been visiting those now deceased to
thank them for being kind to me. They graciously accept my delayed
gratitude.

March 1986

The book of *Psalms*, the *Vedas*, the *Upanishads*, the *Baghavad Gita*,
the *Koran*, and the *Tao Te Ching* were all written by mystics who had
a direct experience of God and the unity of life. However, religions
were created by nonmystics who misunderstood much of the teachings
given by the great ones. Jung was even purported to have said that
religion was a defense against religious experience.

We are all aware of the resulting problems, the most pernicious
being the belief that there is only one true religion. Whether voiced or
unvoiced, that belief has devastating consequences that divide rather
than unite.

One of the most central ideas of objective knowledge
is the idea of the **unity of everything**, of unity in
diversity.[3]

The world is a unity for mystical consciousness and
whose aspect is **universal love**. It is a faculty which all
men have, but few make use of it.[4]

June 1986

Before the group meditation started, I left my body and entered a
deep, rose-colored tunnel. A crystalline form appeared. It had three
unequal axes intersecting at oblique angles. Every facet turned back on

itself. I later learned that it was triclinic. Metaphysically, it represented unity. During this experience, an icy flame passed through me, giving me alternating fevers and chills.

I first saw a web intersected by jewels in April of 1979. These two experiences seem to be related.

Indra's Net, also called Indra's Jewels or Indra's Pearls is a metaphor for the interconnectivity of all phenomena, an experience of some mystics.

Thanks to the theories sprouted by quantum mechanics, mystics are now able to convey their experiences to nonmystics who know something about subatomic concepts, such as nonlocality and connectivity.

June 1986

When I arrived at Florida's Pasadena Palms Hospital, my father was deeply comatose. But because he shared a room, I was unable to stay with him, so I reclined on a bench in the corridor to get some sleep. Several times during the night, a nurse summoned me saying, "Come quickly. He's dying." However, as soon I stood beside his bed, his vital signs improved, and I went back to the bench.

The next day, the nurse, taking pity on me, arranged for him to be moved to a private room. Although he remained comatose, we spent his last day together. I spoke of spiritual things and tried to smooth his transition by using some of the passages I remembered from *The Tibetan Book of the Dead.* That night, my half-brother arrived to sit with me during my father's last hours. We listened as his breathing became intermittent, and when he breathed his last breath, we saw a light leave his body.

After, we drove to our mother's apartment to notify her. She never came to the hospital during his last days. She would say, "He doesn't know I'm there, so why go?"

That evening, the masters filled me with liquid fire and love. They explained, "*We are returning some of the love you gave to him.*"

The next morning, I flew back to California.

This evening, the fragrance of roses is exceptionally strong, but there are no roses in the room. Is my father sending me roses?

December 1986

Until now, my principal focus has been on my spiritual evolution, but tonight, there was a sudden shift. Now I have turned my focus to contributing to God's plan for humanity.

January 1987

Tonight, during our meditation, I felt angel wings embracing me.

March 1987

To understand why I chose to be born to one who rejected me, I decided to try regression. I saw myself very young, unmarried, and forced by my parents to abort the fetus. Had that fetus been my mother?

June 1987

During a full-moon meditation, we were asked to visualize our soul as a lotus. I was the only member of the group who saw a fully opened lotus.

The master explained some of my problems with:

> *You have been passing through the burning ground for several years. We know the stress this puts on your emotional and physical bodies, but it is necessary in order to further purify and upgrade you to withstand **the soon-to-come***

cataclysmic assault on the lower vehicles of humanity. *Some will survive only with the help of disciples; others will be eliminated because of their inability to utilize the transformational forces. Certain disciples will be called upon to modulate or transform the powerful forces about to be released. More group work focused on this transformation will be required. The more workers involved, the less traumatic the result. The mental work most needed is telepathic. Once the transformation is a fact as viewed by us, the physical, emotional, and mental stress will subside in proportion to one's status of karmic debt already paid or expiated. Words do not exactly explain it, but they are close enough. Notice all the signs of growing telepathic awareness. Disregard or discount nothing. Recognition will strengthen belief, and belief will increase reality. The numbers you notice on the clock are another way of indicating to you that all is one. Years ago, the Master Ramana responded to your question "Who are you?" with "We are One." The Master Jesus said, "The Father and I are One," and demonstrated that union by entering your body. Let this truth penetrate your resistant lower mind. You are part of a whole, as is everything on your planet. This truth has not yet reached a critical mass that will precipitate the cosmic leap required of those who are ready. **When a certain percentage***

of humanity realizes this unity, and the critical mass is reached, humanity will take a quantum leap from self-consciousness to soul-consciousness.

December 1987

I don't think that I have ever heard from my Monad before.

You have taken your first step toward the next initiation. I, your Monad, will now have greater control. That all-knowing spark of divinity within is growing in its ability to control your life. Resume your meditation and your reading of esoteric and mystical literature. Your masters are busy with other things, so it is time for you to rely on me, your higher self. I am that which has lived through many incarnations and has retained the lessons learned in each. Ask and you shall receive more of my attention. Know that I also have work to do. Good day.

Was I delusional? My skepticism continued.

Last night, I dreamt of being instructed by the masters. This morning while I was getting ready for work, everything that I did seemed surreal. My body was doing things without conscious control. It was as if the night's instructions were continuing subconsciously.

January 3, 1988—Full Moon of Capricorn

I must keep on working no matter how my body feels. I must be free of reactions. I hear, "*Spirit informs actions; ego informs reactions.*"

Aurobindo speaks of the Monad as the "greater Self."

> In place of the Nature of ignorance…there would be a
> Super Nature of the divine Gnosis and the individual
> would be its conscious…instrument, a participant in
> its action, aware of its purpose and process, aware too
> of its own greater Self.[5]

During group meditation, our leader directed us to try to contact the hierarchy. I left my body, entered an ashram, and was anointed. Filled with love, joy, and bliss, I learned the purpose for this incarnation.

Tonight, I was told to open a certain book and look at the first word that stood out. The word "balance" blew me away. Besides being the first isolated word I heard when I began to meditate, it continued to appear in dreams and messages.

March 1988

Bothered by physical problems and once again feeling sorry for myself, my beloved Master Ramana Maharshi contacted me. It has been five years since I have heard from him.

> *Keep your mind on me. Do not be concerned
> with the physical. It is not really you. It is only
> your vehicle. Remain conscious of your eternal
> self. There is but one soul. Do not renounce the
> world. Renounce its appearance. The true world
> is within.*

When the message ended, I was able to release the pain with his help. How remarkable and wonderful it is to know that he still watches over me.

Between 1896 and 1926, the year I was born, I could have been one of his devotees or even his mother, who died in 1922. He died in

1950.

Though I knew that the heart was on the left side, the master taught me to connect to his heart using the right sides of our chests. Years later, I read that the spiritual heart is on the right, not on the left.

April 1988

When I feel trapped and perplexed about my profession, my marriage, my mysticism, and almost everything, my usual response is to get sick. The Master R. M. uses a delightful analogy to explain.

> *When a spirit is stuck in a small body, it makes trouble like an elephant shut up in a small hut.*

May 1988

I was disgusted with myself for having what I called another "pity party." Poor me. I was never loved in the way I wanted to be loved. The master interrupted my negative feelings with the following:

> *Man cannot give you what you want. It is like asking a sieve to hold water. The love you seek you already have.*

It is hard to believe that the masters are not frustrated with my miserable groveling. I eat to fill a perceived emptiness while I know that I am already filled with the love of God. During our mystical union, Christ made me realize that we were wed in love forever. I weep while I remember the ecstasy of that night. Oh, how ignorant I am. No, not ignorant but forgetful of what I really know to be true.

August 1988

Perhaps Joseph Campbell is right when he says that the only true wisdom can be reached by suffering. "It alone can open the mind to all that is hidden to others."[6]

September 1988

Last night, the room began to spin, so I asked my husband to help me get ready for bed. Though frightened, I remained calm as my limbs began numbing, and a deep sleep overtook me. The next day, I was fine, but I had the distinct impression of being in two places at once. Joseph Campbell described a state of grace as the ability to play here and there at the same time.

January 1989

The symbol for pi, which may have been one of the seven symbols I received some years ago, is the ratio of the circumference of any circle to its diameter. It is a nonrepeating decimal that cannot be specified exactly. Like my chemical formula $AL(OH)3$, it is neither this nor that.

After I recorded a message, I was told that my translation was not always accurate but that it was nevertheless acceptable.

June 1990

Today I retired from teaching to take care of my husband, who has been diagnosed with Non-Hodgkin's lymphoma.

March 1992

For almost two years, I have been too busy with caring for my husband to write in my journal, and my masters have thoughtfully allowed me this time to focus on him.

After several days in bed with various ailments, I decided to call for help. The answer came in the following message:

Your focus on the body and its problems must stop. The body is only your temporary abode. It is not you. Change your thoughts and raise your vibration no matter what is happening to the body.

Drained of energy for several weeks because of many physical and emotional problems, I was surprised when the kundalini suddenly fueled all the chakras and they began to whirl, creating harmonics in every cell and organ of my body. I was instantaneously and completely healed and rejuvenated.

A strong vibration made my teeth chatter.

> The Ida and Pingala are the sharps and flats of the FA of human nature...which when struck in a proper way, awakens the sentries of either side.[7]

During a quivering, I became aware of my etheric body's connection to the chakras. This happened once before during group meditation. I read that the nervous reactions of the disciple, whose etheric body is in close rapport with his nervous system, cannot be explained rationally. When I called upon the masters to modify the stimulation, a shaft of light entered my body, and it relieved me of some stress.

March 1992

A violent shaking warranted my calling upon the master for help. I received a shaft of light that smoothed out the shaking but did not completely eliminate it. The aura of an ashram, an arch of loving light, embraced me. Though these experiences are confusing and often stressful, they infuse me with abundant energy. Other mystics have described the shaking.

> I shook just like a nervous old person.[8]

April 1992

As I looked at my copy of the painting *Opening of the Third Eye* by Mihran K. Serailian, a profound sleepiness overcame me, and although I had just awakened from a very sound night's sleep, I slept for another two hours. This had happened to me many times before. There is something about the head of Minerva showing the pineal and pituitary glands, involved in opening the Third Eye that triggers a profound reaction.

On the morning of the full moon of Aquarius, I quivered for about fifteen minutes.

May 1992

In *Sufi Teachings* by Hazrat Inayat Khan, I read, "**Balance** is the keynote of spiritual attainment."[9]

The masters continue to remind me of the importance of balance, probably because I tend to be out of balance most of the time.

Chapter Seventeen
Lost Love

May 17, 1992

Because chemotherapy was not successful, my husband received his first experimental treatment of monoclonal antibodies. The clinical-trial period was projected to last anywhere from three months to two years, and it could result in the remission of his cancer. But last night's dream of a torn wedding gown, a broken ring, and a funeral warned of a different ending.

July 17, 1992

I had to put a bank account in the trust before my husband died. With the doctor's assurance that he would live for at least three hours after his kidneys failed, and because the trip to the bank would take less than an hour, I left the hospital. After I concluded my business, I opened the safety deposit box to make absolutely sure it was empty. What I saw in the box bore a prophetic message: my husband had just died. After I looked at my watch to note the time and mourned, I returned to the hospital. My husband died at 10:20 AM, twenty minutes before I had returned to the hospital, the exact time that the contents of the safety deposit box had given me the message. The box was empty except for a heavy gold Star of David, the only piece of jewelry my husband owned.

August 1992

A minister friend called to tell me that my husband had telephoned her shortly before his death to say how much he loved me and to ask if she would pray for me. He probably thought that my mysticism would not be acceptable to God.

I was saddened while I read my husband's journals. They revealed a tortured personality, one who kept asking what God meant for him to do. They also revealed how much he loved me, something he had not verbally expressed for many years. I am ashamed to say that while he lay dying, I yearned to hear him say that he loved me. He did not, but he did say, "I don't know what I would have done without you," probably a more meaningful statement, but I still wanted to hear, "I love you."

November 1992

I miss my husband terribly. Despite my upset stomach, nausea, imbalance, restlessness, and a lack of coordination, this Victor Roinson quote made me laugh.

> "Widows are divided into two classes—bereaved and relieved."

I am both bereaved and relieved—bereaved because he is gone, and relieved because we are no longer suffering.

Another message about physical problems:

> *Since disciples are acting as transformers of humanity's negative energy, they will be experiencing many distressing physical symptoms.*

After an electrical tempest passed from my head to my heart, sleep came. At 2:22 AM, dizzy and weak, I endured the familiar shaking.

Numbness slowly crept through my body. Then, a radiant sun came to rest on my heart, and I was healed.

December 1992

During the whole month of November, I suffered emotional and physical pain.

As I started to write, a presence interrupted with the following:

> *If you are distressed by anything external, the pain is not due to the thing itself but to your estimate of it; and this, you have the power to revoke at any moment.*

The masters have told me that this stimulation is required for further spiritual development and for the release from the effects of built-up emotional and mental contamination, which I have been exposed to from internal and external sources. The masters are well aware of my suffering for the sake of "the way," and they tell me that they will ease the stress as much as possible by buffering the forces.

Despite the fact that my transcendental experiences have been proven valid in many ways, my skepticism still causes me to doubt their reality at times.

> Only materialists and atheists never doubt. **Doubt is an integral part of faith**. Doubt is faith's dialectic partner.[1]

My whole body began to shake, and my teeth chattered. My Monad promised that it would stay close to me until I overcame the present confusion.

It has been five months since I lost the great love of my life. Reading his journals puts me in touch with his soul, a soul that I glimpsed from time to time, a soul obscured by a tormented personality.

March 1993

In 1986, I was sick, fearful, and confused. Now seven years later, I am sick, fearful, and confused. The cycles of the expansion of my consciousness are always preceded by periods of illness, fear, and confusion, which I sometimes call "dark night of the soul." The cycle began in 1972. Dark nights appear and disappear suddenly, seemingly without cause, as do moments of rapture.

July 1993

As I felt a numinous presence, I waited expectantly. Someone was pulling on a golden cord that seemed to come out of the top of my head, and a shaft of brilliant golden light entered my head through the cord. This message followed:

> *You must not try to understand. Remain receptive and without thought for the rest of the day.*

August 1993

A sudden weakness in my legs is drawing me into the earth. Three or four earthquakes followed shortly thereafter.

This afternoon, I heard the flutter of wings and felt the movement of air. When I looked around, I saw nothing unusual, so I asked my higher self to explain my experience. She informed me that I was being helped to experience the rhythms of Mother Earth to advance my usefulness to her. A scary answer came from the masters:

> *These dormant instincts are being awakened because they will soon be necessary for survival. We don't need you more active. We need you to stay put for the time being. These are very critical*

*times, and we need all ensouled humans working
with us. We need God's soldiers on earth to be
quietly receptive for further instructions. Remain
where you are and continue your receptivity to
our communication. The body and mind must
remain still. Even your frequent periods of illness
requiring inactivity can be helpful to us, as long
as you do not become preoccupied with and
worry about them. Because of the crisis on your
planet, our contacts will become more frequent.
Choose with care the company you keep, the
foods you eat, and the thoughts you entertain.
Make no effort to expand your social activities or
your acquaintances. We have removed most of
the negative influences from your life. Don't look
for replacements.*

During meditation I experienced the following past life regressions:

After a sudden excruciating pain in my eyes, I drifted back in time and found myself being queried about my visions. Because I had been found guilty of witchcraft, my eyes were being poked out with a burning stick. Later, my body was burned.

I developed a pain in the left side of my head, shoulder, and arm.

I was a French-Canadian fur trapper who had just been bludgeoned and pushed into an icy lake. This was the same type of blow that I had received as Karim, the moneylender.

As the servant of a recently deceased pharaoh, I was about to be buried alive with his court.

I was a young child trying to find my way home after being abandoned in a forest in Germany.

I was a French woman in love with an English pilot during World War I. My second husband had been fascinated by World War I memorabilia, and he had wanted to be a pilot.

Near a lighthouse on the western coast of Ireland, an old woman was sitting in a rocking chair waiting for her seafaring husband who would not return. I later received more. Near death, her grown son and daughter stood beside her bed. At a wake taking place in a tavern, I saw her in a coffin. .

As soon as I asked my spirit to allow me to see my deceased husband, there he was, looking youthful and happy to be with his daughter and his brother. His spirit embraced me with comforting love as he kissed me tenderly. He promised that he would wait for me. I was incredulous when he added that he was sorry for all the pain he had caused me. He continued, "The next time we are together, I will love and protect you." Even more startling was his statement that my love had saved his soul. He thanked me and was gone.

Today has been full of joy. I am finally becoming serious about writing a book about my mystical experiences.

September 1993—Full Moon of Libra

I have been extremely nervous for the past few days. The influx of energy is overwhelming me. Spirit tells me it is available for help in buffering the powerful incoming energies.

Chapter Eighteen
Interlude

October 1993

This afternoon, I went to my husband's doctor to renew one of my prescriptions. This evening, he called to ask me to have lunch with him. In the twenty years I have known him, he has never so much as looked at me in a lecherous way. However, I suspected that the luncheon would probably be a prelude to something more exciting. He knew about my nonexistent sex life, a result of my husband's illness. Despite the guilt I was already feeling because he was married and the fear that a relationship with him would interfere with my spiritual progress, I consented to the lunch.

The lustful interlude lasted for three months.

> *Oh dear child of God, your eyes are being opened to the glory that awaits you when you transcend your present human condition and become divine. I will be there to help you through the tribulations that you are now experiencing. Do not lose faith. We love you and your soul mate (a girlfriend of mine). You both have our blessings. You incarnated together to work with*

people. Never leave each other's sides. Your love for each other increases the power for good.

I cried with gratitude.

Do not weep so, sister. The joy you sometimes experience will increase. Your life is important to us. Remain open to our communication. Quiet your mind so that you can hear clearly and interpret us correctly. We mean to use you. Your soul mate and you are great souls with different perspectives. Both paths are leading to the same place. Come together often so that your soul purposes are strengthened and your insights stimulated. You are one soul that came to do a common work. Whom God has joined together, let no man put asunder. You have been chosen to join the group of humans ready to make the quantum leap in consciousness. Have no fear. You will survive. Your ability to love is precious. Increase your patience and courage. Your tears of joy are an anointing.

My soul mate remarried after her husband's death, and she is presently living in Arkansas. She calls about once a year.

I asked my masters what to do about Dr. T. They answered with the following:

He has entered your life for a reason that you will later realize. Do not send him away. He will leave when it is time. He is still unaware of his spiritual purpose. You will not be contaminated by him. Good day, my loving child.

During the next few weeks I received the following messages:

Never think that you are not worthy of our attention. You have earned what you receive. Stop being so self-critical and self-deprecating. Love thyself as we love thee. Once again, I say good day.

My dear, sweet child, do not inhibit your loving nature. That love comes from us to you and from you to all creatures of the earth. Some may misinterpret your loving nature, but take no heed. You are a natural channel of love. Continue to allow that love to flow from us to you and from you to the world.

Dearly beloved, we have been preparing you for many years to receive these messages. Do you remember that we said you were being prepared for telepathic communication from us? You are prepared. You need only to continue to be a receptive and obedient initiate. You shall be rewarded with more gifts. These early morning hours, when most are still asleep, facilitate our reaching you. Your ability to heal will increase. Writing will become easier. Your loving guides *take turns communicating with you. As you have noticed, there is a marked difference in our manner of speaking. You have earned our trust, and we welcome your help in our effort to transform humanity. Keep your journal beside your bed and await our early morning messages. Thank you for the willingness to align your will with ours.*

Dear, sweet disciple, you are now discovering the power of the mind and the body and the power of kundalini, which was partially released some time ago. Now that your sexuality has been reawakened, kundalini is working its magic. Where your mind is, your power is, and it has now overstimulated you sexually. Do not allow it so much control over your body and mind. Move the sexual energy to the higher chakras, and you will recover your balance. This powerful energy will require control that you never needed before. We reiterate that what you have been experiencing as sexual energy and increased sexual desire is caused by the stimulation and release of the kundalini, which had to be released. You now have experience of its tremendous power. This man has functioned to release the residual kundalini, causing you to lose your balance. The sexual inhibitions that previously existed held back kundalini. Now that your inhibitions are no longer active, the power released is overwhelming your body and mind. You must learn to channel this power for creative use.

You will get help from us through alignment. You will be able to move that powerful energy from place to place as it is needed. Right now, you are out of control, but we will assist you to regain control. The time for using this great power, with a little help from this man, is at hand. Sex is certainly an important part of life on your planet, but you must channel those sexual energies to become more creative and loving and to open your third eye's intuitive and clairvoyant abilities. You have been shocked by the power of this energy. That is good, but remember that it is your power and it can be used in any way you desire. Your spiritual purpose will not be benefited if you waste too much of this precious energy. You may well enjoy this energy while it is below the waist, but remember that your major focus should be on your higher centers. Your most recent sculpture is a presentation of kundalini. This morning as you read "Revelation" by Barbara Marx Hubbard, you realized the possibility of rejuvenation. You have also noticed the rejuvenating qualities of the kundalini. If you think of growing younger rather than older, you will notice the difference. Remember that anything is possible to a "prototype" or an evolutionary. The physical rejuvenation is symbolic.

A poem:

As a youth, I struggled to conform to norms.
Now that I am old, I accept my uniqueness.

The ringing in my right ear was a signal to get ready to receive a message:

> *Sex is the lowest level of love, but it can open the possibility of higher types of love. If creatures had no attraction for one another, how could we ever become one? This man was drawn to you, not only by sexual desire as he supposed. He was always attracted to you, but only now is he free to make his move, because you are a widow. What he doesn't realize is that he is ready to receive something more than sex from you. He mentioned that he felt something mysterious that drew him to you. He wasn't lying. Most men who have been attracted to you have not recognized the magnetism of your aura. When your aura is exhibiting certain vibrations, you will be attractive to anyone who is sensitive to those vibrations. People who are attracted to one another are not aware of subtle energies. You are not only opening sexually but emotionally, mentally, and spirituality. Therefore, you need not worry about this affair. It will not interfere with your spiritual growth, but quite the*

contrary. It will advance your growth. The runes you are being guided to draw are ones that tell you to trust us. Your skepticism is no longer necessary. As the runes indicate, you are rising from the fire of kundalini like the phoenix. The old must be left behind in order to rise again. Little deaths sometimes seem like the big one. The runes have told you to relinquish control of the lower to the higher. What beckons is unknown creative power.

While I was ruminating, another message came to me:

Recognize, dear one, that we will fill you to overflowing with what you need. Not fill, flush. You must always remain open so that there is room for more. Love must flow from us to you and from you to humanity. Don't try to hoard, save, or store what we so freely give. People cannot give what they do not have. Only your equals or superiors can give to you. Give freely of your love. Love and release. Expect nothing in return. You are pouring out love to all who enter your life. Think of a production line. Pour out your blessings to those who are passing through your life. Do not hold up the flow. Give and release. You are here to give, not to expect. Remember the central purpose of your life is to be a channel of love and wisdom or light. Men enter love through sexual experience; women use sex to get love. Women bear the seed of love in their hearts when they are born. It germinates as they grow spiritually, and when it flowers, those near will receive it, whether plant, animal, child, man, or woman. Whoever is near a flower is free to smell its fragrance; whoever is near a flower-soul is free to partake of love. People in need have been arriving at your doorstep all of your life. You answered the call of your parents, freely gave yourself, and entered the womb. But do not misunderstand. Not everyone who enters your life is in need; sometimes you are in need, and people are sent to answer your need. What you need in order to learn and grow may come in many forms: people, books, special events, lectures, trips, or guides and masters. Your next assignment is to start monitoring your thoughts. Negative thoughts are to be dispelled. Many of them are not yours but those of the collective.

November 1993

Men have something to teach you, but it may not necessarily be something you expect. Try to keep your mind on us despite the distractions. Your attention and receptivity is especially essential at this time. Let them come and go without too much concern. Contemplate humanity working together peacefully for the good of the planet. You waste precious energy thinking of the past and future. Keep your mind in the present. Talk to yourself lovingly. Let things happen. Stop all that frantic planning and activity. Think not for the morrow, dear, sweet soul. We will take care of that. Visualize all of the people on your planet working together peacefully for the good of the planet. Keep your mind on what is happening in the moment, please. You have noticed the repetitive nature of our communications. There are two reasons for this: The first reason is our desire for you to learn quickly and retain what is learned. The second I have already indicated— there are several of us communicating with you. Although we are aware of what you need to learn, we have different ways of saying it, and repetition is necessary for memory. A change of consciousness is imminent when a critical mass is reached. Spread the word as often as you can. The more people who have that thought, the more quickly the change.

Tomorrow I am leaving for Australia.

While I was looking out of the window of a tour bus in Australia, I saw many instances of the future:

- A proliferation of homosexuality leads to nonsexual unions.
- Sexual intercourse is no longer needed to create life.
- People are attracted to each other's spirituality.
- We learn how to consciously control our bodies.
- We become co-creators with God.
- We dematerialize and rematerialize, like the characters in *Star Trek*, whenever we want to go someplace.

The vision ended, and I was told that I would become clairvoyant to increase my healing ability.

> This personal or subjective way of seeing and knowing reality is impossible to communicate except by using symbols, analogies, and metaphors. Since this way of knowing is essentially impossible to convey, it is seen by those to whom it is described, as occult, obscure, bizarre, and even absurd.[1]

December 1993

Because I was very conflicted about my relationship with Dr. T. and wondered how I could end it, I heard the following:

> *You knew from the onset that this wasn't a relationship that you wanted to continue for long. It has served its purpose. End it now.*

This was a most emphatic statement, but it seemed to contradict a previous message.

> *Why be curious about other things when you don't even know yourself.*

There are two kinds of people: those trying to learn about themselves and those trying to escape learning about themselves.

August 1994

My deficiencies suddenly loomed large, and I began to doubt my goodness. Seeing yourself objectively can be demoralizing.

Chapter Nineteen
Spiritual Progress

January 1995

Well, I didn't have to end the affair, because the doctor did. He must have gotten the master's message.

The following message was exceptionally surprising:

> *Tomorrow, you will receive something that will surprise you. It will come to you telepathically from us. We need you to speed up your spiritual progress. It is critical at this time. Open yourself to our communication. Put aside your concerns and interests. Do not be afraid of opening yourself to automatic writing. We will surely keep you safe, as you are ours. Your path was set eons ago. Never doubt. Our language may seem strange to you, but let it flow. The handwriting may become illegible, but allow the scribbles and continue to write as we are dictating. Open yourself. You no longer need to fear. Master Koot*

Hoomi needs you to make every effort to raise your vibration by thinking only positive thoughts and doing only positive things. With a sufficiently high vibration, you will be able to withstand the onslaught of negativity that is coming. The world is in a state of chaos. We need those of you who have come into manifestation at this time to follow us in faith and not to expect to understand everything. Your intellect will only interfere. Only those of like mind and of sufficiently high vibration will be able to survive the vibratory changes needed to purify the consciousness of humanity. Remember, keep your thoughts pure and follow the guidance we give. You will be able to continue doing the daily tasks that are necessary, but do not fill your time with that which is not essential for our purpose. Do not begin any new activities unless directed by us. You have already made a commitment to serve. Thoughts are creative, so unless you are sure they will create good, stop thinking them. We will fill your mind with creative thoughts if you allow it. The thoughts we give are crucial. We respect your skepticism, and we will eventually answer all of your questions. We will correct you when necessary. Love and purity are critical. Do not allow thoughts of self-gratification or self-pity to take hold of you.

You want to know about your husband. He is learning some of the lessons that he failed to learn on earth. He is hard-headed, as you well know. Be assured that you did your best to enlighten him, but you did not realize that words and preachment do no good when one is not ready. Bless you for trying, though. All anyone can do is to be a good example and not allow another to affect or infect one. Do what you can for those who enter your life, but do not allow anyone to deter you from your preordained destiny. You should continue to give away what you do not really need. Your possessions will only burden you and interfere with our plans for you.

Recite "The Great Invocation" every day at noon while you visualize light, love, and the will of hierarchy.

Benjamin Creme's timing of the return of Christ was off, but indeed, Christ has incarnated and is waiting for a critical mass of humanity to respond to his vibration with love and compassion. Give to others what you will, but first and foremost, give yourself to us as you have always done.

Do not worry. Keep your thoughts productive and co-creative, or don't think. Many are destroying life with their thoughts and actions. Our beloved ones must set themselves apart and take no part in humanity's self-destructiveness. Again, do not worry. Keep your thoughts and actions creative, which will help us to transform human consciousness. That is all for now.

After this lengthy and wonderful message, while I wondered why I was told that this message would come tomorrow when it came today, I was told: "*There is no linear time.*"

"The Great Invocation" is a world prayer that Tibetan Master Djwhal Khul transmitted to Alice Bailey. (See Endnotes.)

The Great Invocation

From the point of Light within the Mind of God
Let light stream for into the minds of men
Let Light descend on Earth.

From the point of Love within the heart of God
Let love stream forth into the hearts of men
May Christ return to Earth.

From the Center where the Will of God is known
Let purpose guide the little wills of men
The Purpose which the Masters know and serve.

From the Center which we call the race of men
Let the Plan of Love and Light work out
And may it seal the door where evil dwells.

Let Light and Love and Power restore the Plan on Earth.

Krishnamurti said: "I beheld Lord Maitrya, and Master K. H."[1]

The Ashram of the Master K. H. is the presiding Ashram owing to the fact that it is a second ray **love/ wisdom ashram, and therefore upon the same line of energy as that of the Christ himself.**[2]

It is also written that Master K. H. will assume the role of the world teacher when Christ moves on to higher and more important work. (With tongue in cheek, I say, "What could be more important than us?")

My whole body began to shake, and my teeth chattered.

January 1995

In response to my appeal for a buffer of the powerful energies from Shambhala, I was told that I could temporarily visualize myself surrounded by a shell of light. Several years ago, I was directed not to shield myself.

March 1996

The masters tell us we must change.

> *This is a time of great change, not only for you but for your whole planet. Humanity must change. Your loss of interest in the worldly and the emptiness you feel is not depression but the spiritual detachment necessary for the growth of the soul. Stay in the light. Don't let darkness overwhelm you. You have been so inculcated with concepts of what the world considers reality that when you start to break through that shell into a world of light and love, you necessarily will feel lost and empty. Remember, unless you are empty, you cannot be filled. You will never be abandoned by those who love you. You will be supported in everything you do for our sake. We will help with the book that you must write in order to bring mystical reality out of the closet.*

Your faith in us and your steadfastness will soon be rewarded with more inspiration, guidance, and love than you can imagine. The immediate physical problems can be endured. They are only significant from a spiritual perspective and will not threaten your life. Rejoice in the mysticism that you are privy to.

The rule of conscious obedience to the higher truth of the spirit, the surrender of the whole being to the light and power that comes from the Supernature, is a second condition which has to be accomplished slowly and with difficulty by the being itself before the supramental transformation can become at all possible.[3]

I wonder why some people have spiritual guidance and mystical experiences while others have little or none. Perhaps it is a matter of awareness and the willingness to participate, or perhaps some may have prepared for a spiritual awakening during previous incarnations. Those who ask for guidance will surely receive it.

The world in which you live is, in fact, an illusion created by agreement amongst yourselves. The world that you, my dear, are glimpsing is the real. Desire is the clue. Desire the worldly, and you get the worldly; desire the realm of spirit, and you get that. The desire, the thought, the word, and the manifestation, in that sequence, things are created.. First comes the desire. Then thoughts begin to dwell, become words and thus the manifestation of the desire is created.

April 1996

During a walking meditation, strong devotional impulses started me crying and wishing to renounce the world in favor of the reclusive life. Was this coming from memories of ascetic past lives? I asked the master if my physical problems might be assaults from the "dark side." Was it possible that disciples could be attacked by dark forces to deter their spiritual progress?

The master answered:

> *I told you that you had a "work" that was planned lifetimes ago. Now, at last, you are ready to undertake this work. It will be difficult, but you will be guided.*

That doesn't answer my question about dark forces, and what is this work I am ready for?

In *Letters on Occult Meditation*, the Dark Brotherhood and the means they use to obstruct the spiritual progress of disciples is explained.[4]

September 1996

I have an intimation that I must no longer rely on the masters but rather turn to my own spirit or monad.

> *The time of the receptive mystic is past, and the time of the white magician is here to serve the race and to convert pure scientific knowledge into the love of divine revelation. The mystic is necessarily becoming the occultist, combining mind and love.*

Because I know that thoughts are creative, I am working at

monitoring my thoughts. I remembered the message I received in March that foretold of a time of great change for humanity. It also suggested that what I called "lethargy" may, in fact, be the detachment necessary for spiritual growth.

August 1996—Full Moon of Virgo

Talk to everyone in his own language. Polarity is eliminated when you become the Buddha. Accept everything as the unfolding of the absolute teaching. Do not follow convention. Follow your inner guidance.

January 1997

In answer to my question about whether I should continue writing this book or not, the spirit entered my body with a high-pitched sound and a tremor and said, "Yes!" The answer to my question about whether or not I should continue the study of mythology was also yes.

I asked what to do about the disturbed young woman I have been trying to help. The answer was: *"Stop trying to save her from her self-created problems."*

All of the people you are trying to save are distracting you from your purpose. Continue your creative activities: writing, painting, sculpting.

An attack of supraventricular tachycardia (i.e., a very rapid heart beat) sent me to the hospital. I was given an infusion to restore regular rhythm. Was the SVT brought on by the energies that so often assault my body?

February 1997

Yesterday, a powerful presence kept me in a sort of stupor. Today, I asked, "What happened?"

The answer was the following: "*You were being magnetized.*"

July 1997

This morning, for no apparent reason, God's love flooded my being, and ecstatic tears washed my face. I tried reading, but I couldn't, because I was half out of body and disoriented. "What is going on?" I asked.

No answer came.

I went to the computer to write, and "Wake up" was the only thing I could type. "I am awake," I affirmed.

I have had all kinds of physical problems for the past few months. Today, I sat at the computer and heard, "Write the book," over and over again. I felt schizophrenic, as if the self, that part of me that has continuity of consciousness and access to all the memories of previous or simultaneous incarnations, had taken over. It was in command. All barriers of forgetfulness were breaking down, and I was becoming all that I had ever been.

October 1997

For months, I have been detached from everything. My life seems meaningless, yet I am not depressed. The emptiness is like a small death.

While I was watching teeming life in what we think of as empty space, my body experienced a jolt.

You will receive guidance infused with love
and light so that you may fulfill your destiny.

Hot tears spilled down my cheeks.

When I heard a ringing in my right ear, my knees buckled. My body shook, and my eyes were not able to focus. A crescendo of energy inscrutably gave me a strong resolve to share my experiences in a book.

Chapter Twenty
Problems

December 1997

Once again, the holidays find me feeling unloved, looking for love from my friends, and struggling with self-pity. How pathetic and ungrateful. I blame myself for all the negativity I feel. Some of the negativity is not mine but humanity's.

A friend took me to the hospital because I had a recurrence of SVT. After another infusion to restore the heart's normal rhythm, I was given a prescription that I was asked to take regularly to prevent further attacks.

January 1998

I asked for healing and was told the following:

> *You will be healed by the renewing of your mind. There is nothing wrong with you. You cannot run away from yourself. Let not your heart be troubled. Lean thou only upon God. You must meditate twice a day during these stressful times. Also, pray and expect to receive what*

you pray for. You are not transforming negative energy. You are absorbing it.

February 1998

We told you that the transformation would make you more sensitive, more aware. You need to practice a new kind of self-control that humanity will need. Part of this is learning to control your body. Every time we give humans more energy, things go haywire. Look at the multitude of problems with sex and food. Animals are not profligate. They kill only what they need, not what they want. They have estrus, which controls their sexual drive. Look what humanity has done with these two freedoms. You are still struggling with your inability to say no to things you shouldn't eat. We need as many prototypes as we can get to make that quantum leap in consciousness. You accepted our grace, but you aren't fulfilling your duty. When you make the transition, you will need great control of the mind and the will in order to stay on the right path to go where you want to go rather than where your scattered self takes you. Because I, your higher self and spirit, took over for your masters, the messages come from me. My messages are not as exotic. Therefore, you take little heed. The snarling wolf that you just imagined as you closed the light is your ego telling you what you want to hear. Listen to me. I will tell you what you need, not what you want. You've got to start listening to, loving, and respecting me, your spirit, as you did your masters. I know your history, all of your lives. You need to move to a new community, not to escape yourself but to spread the spiritual message. People no longer come to you, so you must go to them. Start a meditation group. Bring those close to transition the messages they need. Go for it. Don't dawdle. The time is right. Start dumping your stuff and go. You have just had an example of how easy it is to change your vibration. Listen to me, and you won't have to struggle accepting higher vibrations in the lower vibrational body. You will not feel nervous if you match the vibration by listening to me.

I am so confused by all this. Where do I go, and what do I do?

Don't look back, or you will become a pillar of salt frozen in time. Take any path rather than remaining fixed in the past. Do anything new, break free, move on, and run like a fearless child into the field of violets and buttercups. The violet chooses to shrink from the light of the sun. The buttercup reflects its golden light. Fear not. Step forward. Any path is better than the past that holds you fearfully frozen. Dissolve and flow.

An entity cleared my head of negativity and reminded me to keep pure and loving thoughts. I was directed to hold healing thoughts for a particular person whom I have not seen for many years. As I visualized Cathy surrounded by light and love, I recalled a time when she was hospitalized with hepatitis. One of her friends spurred me into action by saying, "If you expect to see her alive, you had better get to the hospital today." Although she was not a close friend, that evening after work, I hurried to the hospital. As I ignored the warnings about contagion coming from her relatives, who were all lined up against the wall as far away from her as they could get in the room, I went directly to the bed and took her hand. Spirit spoke through me then. I kissed her and left. The next day, she was in recovery.

I remembered another time years after the above incident when Cathy, another friend and I were in Palm Springs. One evening, Cathy turned to me for help because her leg was swelling and turning blue. I simply stroked the leg once or twice, and it was healed. She must have had some divine protector who was using me

Told that another master would instruct me in healing at a distance, I waited anxiously.

March 1998

Years ago, some part of me was liberated. In exaltation, she sang, "I'm free at last." After that, she quickly added, "You can call whenever you need me," and away she flew. I remembered Master R. M. telling me that I no longer had an astral body, but I doubted that it was the astral body that gleefully celebrated her liberation. It may have been the soul.

Even though it has been many years since our mystical marriage, the Christ presence was so powerful tonight that the bed shook. My heart raced, and my body was on fire. Afraid that I might see bloody stigmata, I hesitated before I looked down at my hands. *"Ah, sweet mystery of life, at last I've found thee"* played over and over in my head, and despite my fear, I had to laugh at what I thought was an insensitive joke. I calmed down, fell asleep, and awoke a short time later, disoriented and weak. The crown chakra was once again opening.

As I was pondering yesterday's mysterious happenings, I saw

upraised arms holding a tiny baby. It was me as a newborn. Someone was teasing me with another joke. I had had many memories of previous or simultaneous lives, but never before had I seen myself as a baby. The humorous display lifted me out of my usual serious frame of mind.

In the quotes below, Krishnamurti speaks of the "transcendent personality" as being humorous and capable of an independent existence. If he is right, that may have been the part of me that, years ago, was thrilled that she had finally won her freedom, the one who now was using humor to tease me.

> Having achieved its maturity, the **transcendent personality,** though still connected with the nature which is the source of itself, becomes **capable of independent existence** and may go and come as it pleases through the numberless gateways of consciousness.[1]

> You may meet your own transcendent personality as one gentle creature, slightly **humorous,** very human, childlike in simplicity, but old as the world in wisdom.[2]

An emanation brings a sense of wonder that unites me with all creation, and my consciousness expands giving me greater awareness.

April 1998

Overflowing with joy, I recognize that truth cannot be reached by thought. It is not inscrutable, but words cannot denote it. How can I possibly communicate to others what cannot be expressed or understood even by me, the one who is experiencing? It is required.

I felt less weird after I read *Krishnamurti's Notebook.* He spoke of excruciating headaches, weakness, and sudden surges throughout his body that caused shaking. He claims that these painfully disturbing experiences had to be endured without question or resistance of any kind.[3]

While I was being pulled out of my body by a strong vortex of energy, my ego-personality struggled to maintain control. It eventually lost, and I was off again on another out-of-body journey.

As in the past, nothing seems to hold my interest. I swing from moments of transcendent joy to longer periods of emptiness. All interest in the mundane is swept away, and I wonder how my physical body can be sustained without my attention.

> *Sorry, but you will have to go through this alone. Nobody you know will be able to understand what is happening, but I assure you that all is well. What is called for now is blind faith. We are using you to create a new evolutionary pattern for humanity. It is not necessary for you to understand at this time. Just bear with us and fear not.*

My mind and body are expanding with the universe, and I am becoming infinite.

As a child, I was afraid to go to bed at night because when I was drifting off to sleep, my little body would expand and finally lose its edge.

Spacey, weak, hypersensitive, my pulse, temperature, and blood pressure erratic, enduring continual headaches, how can I hold on to some stability as they work me over, inconsiderate of my fragility?

March, April, and May are my most mystically active months, probably because they are celebrated as the most potent full moons of the year: Aires, Taurus, and Gemini This afternoon, the headache was so bad that I called upon my masters to shield me. Immediately, I was bathed in love, and my headache was gone.

May 1998

> *You are being used for the good of all, not*

for your comfort or benefit. We will do our best to soften the shock to your physical body, which will be required to reach a higher vibration than is comfortable. Do not dissipate our thrust by sharing with your friend. Her vibration has been lowered by her husband and her hyperactivity. You need to control the joy and excitement you feel when we contact you. Reaching out to others at this time only weakens the link.

I am glad you are finally awake. You have had a difficult passage; but finally, another veil has been lifted, and I am better able to reach you.

You have not found your voice yet. Form new positive patterns in your life. Find new things to do and new ways to do old things. Don't get locked in old ruts and patterns that block your flow. Expand your horizons, be courageous, and be open. Think of me, your master. My lips move, but I am voiceless until you find a voice for me. I will find my voice through you. I feel your love, and I know you feel mine. I will always support and protect you even from your own negative tendencies, such as eating imprudently and becoming stuck in negative thought patterns. You have been making some headway in blocking negative thought forms. Good. When the clock awakens you by flashing like numbers, take out your journal. I want to communicate with you in our now-voiceless, telepathic way, the way of your training. This way takes less energy. It is as your Chinese Master told you. Coming down to the earthly sphere is uncomfortable and unnecessary when we have a chela who can receive our thoughts from our place of comfort. The years of preparation are now paying off. Get back to your book. I will be there to help. Your recent experience of vibration is another way of reminding you that I am once again actively making contact. This is the time for you to produce a product of that training. The book must be written. That is why Twitchell's book "Dialogues with the Master" was dropped before you.

He wrote, and so will you. But you will receive me telepathically, not physically. Your health and vitality will be restored. Don't be so willing to believe in your limitations. They are only false beliefs that you use as excuses for not living freely and courageously. Limit your encounters with others, especially now that you have this book to write. We need you to get the more Catholic (universal) message out. You have begun to realize how thoughts create. Your thoughts of physical limitations are creating limitation. Stop and create health and spiritual wealth. Healthy thoughts of strength throughout your body and subconscious will create a new body, a body that you will need to face the new millennium. You created this house as a teenager. You now will be able to have things you dwell on more quickly. Most of your manifestations were created subconsciously. Now start creating consciously. A prime example of manifesting health immediately was the time you rejected the diagnosis of rheumatoid arthritis. You changed the thoughts and behaviors that were crippling your body. You became well and sustained the thought of health for many years. Now, once again, you are falling into thoughts of physical weakness and ill health. Decide right now that you are strong and healthy, and it will be manifested.

May 1998

Today, things long-forgotten are remembered. As I type from my journals, a more accurate word will pop into my head, as if someone is correcting me.

It is 3:33 AM, and the left side of my body is vibrating while consciousness is drifting off. The vibration continues but only on the left side of my body. This has never happened before, as far as I can recall.

Bentov calls "the Physio-Kudalini Syndrome" a "fine-tuning of the nervous system." He notes many symptoms, too. The following are those that I have experienced from time to time: "clairvoyance, clairaudience, healing abilities, headaches, states of bliss, pains on the left side of the body, tingling in the arms or legs, hot hands, leg cramps, heavenly music, problems with vision, showers of light coming out of the top of the head, involuntary movements of the body, hearing high-pitched sounds, musical notes, ecstatic feelings, sexual stimulation, anesthetized left side of the body, knee pain, hip pain, lower back pain, migraines, thyroid disorders, heartbeat irregularities, excessive nervous tension, and depression."[4]

A note (D) played over and over in my right ear, creating a vibration that lasted for about five minutes.

June 1998

Tearfully, I prayed to leave the physical body and return to the unified field. My prayer was partially answered when everything dissolved into a swirling field of energy, the energy of life before physical manifestation.

The following poem was transmitted:

> Oh, dearest God, how often I speak to Thee.
> I weep, yearning for your presence.
> How often I beseech Thee for another moment of
> annihilation, a moment of bliss, without duality,
> a moment of omniscience.
> I pray for another such illuminating moment.
>
> My love for you is greater than my love for all
> that this world has to offer.
>
> Yet, while longing for you,
> I realize we are One now and forever.
> Christ demonstrated this by entering my body,
> soul, and spirit.
> He knew that my skepticism and density
> required the most realistic demonstration.
> Words were not enough for me.
> I had to have a mystical marriage.
>
> The illumination and the marriage sustain
> and enable me to continue the struggle while
> I long for nonduality.
>
> The guidance given by those who serve
>   on your behalf evokes peals of gratitude.

The love we seek on earth can never be found.
Love cometh from God, Creator of all.
Sadly, once again, the serpent of duality
slithers back into my consciousness,
separating us.

July 1998

Flooded with insights and overflowing with ecstasy, tears fell like rain. My ordinary consciousness could not contain such rapture, so I went to my bed and allowed it to suffuse my totality. After a nap, I tried to work, but I was unable to maintain wakefulness. When I found myself out of the body, I asked my customary question: "What is happening?"

There was no answer.

It didn't help to understand that I was never really alone and that feeling alone and isolated was common to all mystics. Although nothing specific was disturbing me, I seesawed from restless activity to profound lethargy. The body had become sensitive to everything, and I was beside myself, literally and figuratively.

October 1998

One of the messengers told me that the chiropractic treatments and massage that I have been receiving is stimulating kundalini, causing excessive heat and shaking.

I was reminded to keep an empty mind to enable transmissions.

My shortcomings unfurled before me. Submerged negative thoughts and feelings bubbled up and weighed me down. As I surrendered, an instant transformation took place. An all-knowing, eternal being emerged from the depths, the Self.

Recently, I leave the house feeling great and come home with aches and pains. Am I absorbing humanity's pain? In Santa Barbara, I was able to transform negative energy in the form of pain. "You, master, have told me that I am a transformer of energy. Why am I absorbing so much negativity?"

Excessive self-criticism caused me to sink into another dark night of the soul, nullifying spiritual progress.

November 1998

For several weeks, I have been hearing a voice repeating, "*You are going to meet a man.*"

I always respond, "Oh, no, not another man. I don't want to meet a man." Trying to suppress or ignore the voice didn't help. It simply continued. My voices had never misled me, so I began looking for him wherever I went.

At October's meeting of an art association, just before the demo was about to begin, a latecomer arrived and sat next to me. That was not unusual, because I was sitting in the first row near the door, which made that seat most easily accessible to a latecomer. After the break for refreshments, the man returned to the seat beside me and initiated a conversation about art, of course.

The following month's meeting couldn't come soon enough for me. By now, though still not wanting another man in my life, I was certainly caught up in the intrigue. Nevertheless, I would have to wait a whole month for the next chapter of the mystery to unfold, and I was ready, not for romance but for adventure.

Just in case the man I met last month was the one, I arrived for the November meeting with my name, address, and phone number on a card. The latecomer took the vacant seat beside me, this time carefully guarded. During our break for refreshments, I checked him from time to time as he chatted with what seemed to be every young woman in the room. How could he possibly be interested in a seventy-two-year-old woman, even though he was probably about my age? Rather soon after he returned to his seat, he asked not just for my phone number but for a date. We later went to an art reception in Laguna.

After several so-called dates, things became more serious. He seemed perfect—handsome, intelligent, artistic, financially solvent, and most importantly, spiritual. (He had been a minister.) The only problem was that his wife had died only sixteen months before our meeting. What came as a complete surprise to both of us was how quickly we fell in love. (Because this is not a romance novel, I will not go into the details of the push and pull of our relationship.) Confused about loving two women at once, his dead wife and lively me, he started seeing a therapist. He ended our relationship rather abruptly after six months.

As the relationship had been foretold by my voices, I had mistakenly assumed that it would have led to marriage. However, the voices hadn't told me that I needed another painful experience to hasten my spiritual development. This had obviously been an opportunity created to teach me to love unconditionally, to resolve my childhood abandonment issues, and to know that I didn't need a man to love and fulfill me.

Unloved and abandoned as a child, anyone who paid attention to me seemed acceptable. I was not discriminating. Many boys and men were attracted to me, but the man who became my first husband was the first one to propose marriage.

I was nineteen, and he was a divorced thirty-three-year-old. I accepted his proposal for three reasons as I can recall: First, he said he loved me. Second, he seemed so unattractive and unlovable that I was sure he would be very happy to have me as a wife and therefore would come straight home every evening after work. The third reason that I accepted his marriage proposal was a need to get away from the fights between my mother and my alcoholic stepfather. These were certainly not good reasons to marry. However, a nineteen year-old brain does not usually have the ability to make good judgments because it has not fully matured. As the saying goes, I went from the frying pan into the fire. My prospective husband, unbeknown to me, turned out to be an alcoholic, too.

March 1999

Today, at about 11:00 AM, that strange, sudden sleepiness overcame me, indicating that something was about to happen. Inside a chrysalis, my caterpillar body was being consumed by the ideational cells of a butterfly. Then, suddenly, there was a cracking, and I emerged as a huge white butterfly.

April, 1999—Easter Morning

As I languished after another painful abandonment, I wrote a letter to the man who entered by life as had been predicted. I thanked him for bringing love and excitement into my forlorn life, for allowing me to share his life if even for a moment, and for enabling me to learn some very important things about myself. He answered with a phone call, thanking me for the letter and declaring his love. He said that he also learned much from our relationship. We were brought together because we each needed healing.

> The heart is clearly the single organ that needs
> wounding and sacrifices ... it is the closing of the
> heart far more than the closing of the mind that keeps
> folk from transformation and deepening.[5]

When I felt the trembling that usually preceded a message, I put down the book I was reading. After I adjusted my chair to face northeast, I heard the following:

It does not matter which way you face. What you are experiencing is creative energy, which is true life, the life that the body experiences as living is only a part of the total life energy of the universe. When the body dies, life does not end. That same life energy fills a less physical form in which you still exist. You will always exist. The Gnostic Gospel is closer to the truth than the orthodoxy of most churches. Only the spiritually initiated have any inkling of reality, and even they have only a glimmer. There are many veils to lift before one can see the magnificence. It is unknown in your present form. The great mystery is well beyond cognition. Do not try to interpret these words or even try to dilute them with your limited understanding. We are gifting you to the limit of your capacity to understand or receive. Take our words as they come to you whether they make sense or not. You are an initiate of lowly rank who needs to learn much. Your impulsive nature must be controlled before you can be upgraded. Do not act impulsively but await guidance. Ask, and it shall be given unto you. Express love, not egotistic thoughts and actions. We are the guides who monitor your spiritual progress. We recognize the turmoil you have been experiencing as a result of this man we placed in your life. He can be a powerful teacher if you see through his individuation or specificity. You have already become aware of some of the lessons to be learned in relation to him. He need not even be present for you to learn from him. He is just a symbolic presence to bring you more self-awareness. Your love for him opened you, enabling us greater heart approach. Love enables us to reach you. Your path is one of love—love tempered by wisdom. Whether this man physically reenters your life or not is not important, but what you can learn as a result of the love you are experiencing is very important. We needed to open your heart again. What you fill yourself with is self-destructive. Fill yourself with our love and nourishment, and become your true self.

We told you he was coming, but we didn't tell you why. He was needed for you to have the insight and pain that you are now experiencing. We didn't intend for you to get stuck with him. Remember the analogy of the factory with its moving belt that carries people in and out of your life. Don't hold on to anyone. Don't desire. Life is transitory, not reality, not stability, but constant movement, change. You can't hold on to anything. Experience and learn from what comes, and then let it go. Be in the now. It allows you to have an experience of other's realities. Everything you think you have actually has you. The hook and line of fishing has two ends—you and your fish have each other. This man holds on to the dead; you hold on to the living. He will let go before you will if you don't recognize your predicament. When the fish is dead, you throw it back. While it is alive, you are responsible for keeping it alive or killing it and letting go. This man was the big hook we chose, because he was not ready for your power. We knew he would withdraw, allowing you to face yourself in a new way. If he comes back into your life, you will not be as needy and vulnerable. You need your freedom to live in the center of what you perceive as your mystery. You must remain unattached. Live alone. Don't marry again. Don't get too deeply involved with anyone. Love and let go. Serve but do not give yourself away. You are not a sacrificial object; you are our subject on the way to becoming a ,master. Don't get ego involved with us or anyone. Your ego must not lead. It must be recognized for what it is—part of being human. But you, who are in the process of transformation, need to sublimate the lower instincts, thoughts, and feelings.

Your home is with us, now only in consciousness, later with us in body. Detachment is what you are learning. We used him because you are most attached to loving and being loved. What you are realizing is that your true joy is with us, not with what the world offers and withdraws. We never withdraw our love. You withdraw from us. By letting go of your seemingly insatiable need for love, you will escape the world's hold on you. We need you free and unattached. We need to be the center of your life. We are what you are seeking, and you don't yet realize it. If you go to plays, paint, have friends, travel, or whatever, it doesn't matter as long as you see these things as dalliances, not especially meaningful.

Chapter Twenty-One
Balance

May 1999

As I plummeted into an oceanic instability that was both physical and emotional, I was told, "Reread *A Course in Miracles.*"

This morning, puzzled by an unsteadiness that had me running into walls, I returned to bed and slept for another couple of hours. Though I didn't remember what had happened several hours before, I jumped out of bed. My balance was restored, and I heard the following:

True balance is now attained. You are transformed by the renewing of your mind. You have been doing God's work your whole life, accepting those who feel guilty and unlovable and bringing them back to self-love, which is the love of the spirit of God within. Now you are able to love unconditionally. You need to realize that having a man in your life does nothing to fulfill you. Only God's love and grace can fulfill. Since your husband's death, you have, of necessity, been caught up in worldly concerns. Now is the time for you to make the biggest transformation of your life. Realize you need no one to fulfill you. You are already perfect as God made you. Study "A Course in Miracles", and when your mind wanders, fill it with the lessons in this course and think of me, Christ, who demonstrated our union. Also, remember your Master Ramana, who answered your question with "We are One."

May 1999

While I absent mindedly watched my image getting larger and larger as I approached a mirror in the hall, I suddenly realized that I was not getting larger, but smaller. My real self is much larger than the lesser me, who inhabits the physical body. Because I felt trapped, I shed tears of compassion for my lesser self. A searing pain penetrated my heart. For the first time, not mentally, not emotionally, but in the deepest way possible, I realized that I was confined by the body, its emotions, thoughts, and beliefs. I wished for freedom while I became poignantly aware that I had chosen this body as my temporary prison.

Einstein testified to moments when one feels free from one's own identification with human limitation.

If I've never been bound, I can never be liberated. How could I think that the Self is restricted to formlessness or imprisoned by form?[1]

I am now responding to a very strong impulse to write.

Today, a new consciousness is being born. It will be what Sri Aurobindo called the super-consciousness. It will usher in the new millennium. Not everyone will be able to express this new form. This will be a consciousness that recognizes the oneness of mankind. It will recognize the oneness of nations. It will free man of his ego's sense of individuality. The soul of mankind will be in ascendance. The ego no longer reigns.

More people will be having so-called mystical experiences. They are not really mystical, but experiences of a reality of which most men know nothing. These experiences will be accepted just like our sensory experiences. Men will openly share these experiences and begin to understand their import. The metaphysical will become as commonplace as the physical is now. Mankind will lose its fear of "the other" and of the unknown. It will accept the fact of evolution as a continuing phenomenon. It will also accept and recognize guides and masters who come from other dimensions to help it evolve. It will have such control over physical manifestation that it will be able to dematerialize and rematerialize. Mankind will be able to travel to other worlds and other dimensions .You will be experiencing the love, joy, and bliss, not rarely but often.

Once you have finished the first rewrite of the book, I will work with you to prepare the manuscript for mailing to publishers. Right now, you need to sit down every day to write. At times, I will be introducing ideas or words. As you work, maintain a meditative openness that will allow me to communicate. You, with perseverance and desire, will now be able to allow your soul to take command of your life.

Don't act impulsively. Ask your soul if whatever you are about to do is what it would want. Guard your thoughts carefully. Many thoughts that you think are your own are not. Don't accept them and certainly do not follow their lead in thoughts or actions. Let them flit in and throw them out as you do during meditation. Do not invite them in and entertain them.

Your master has summoned me to aid you in the writing of this book and the preparation of the manuscript. No need to know who I am. I will infuse you with the desire to write. Respond to the impulse that I put into your mind. I may be available at times when you least expect to be writing, but hearken to my call and go to the computer and await my direction. That is all I have to say for now. You may continue what you were doing before I called.

Chapter Twenty-Two
A Major Move

December 12, 2000

Today, I left the home that my husband and I had designed and built thirty-three years ago, a home the nomadic child dreamed of as she walked the streets at dusk, imagining that in every brightly lit window lived a happy, loving family, a home the romantic sixteen-year-old started building in her mind, a home that grew as she grew.

For several months, I had been helping a friend look for a retirement home, but when we found one that we both liked, she did not move in. I did. I had never considered moving before. In fact, I had just spent a great deal of money improving my house; however, when a message from beyond told me that I should move, I consented without a second thought. How could I leave the home I had longed for since I was a child, the home that I thought I could not live without, the home that I believed would fill my emptiness, the home that grounded me? How could I leave without a twinge of pain, without ever looking back with nostalgia? How could that possibly be? The answer was simple but enigmatic. My masters had wiped the emotional slate clean, the slate on which this house had become the home that held all of my dreams and fantasies.

When I was told to move, I only had one question: "What am I supposed to do in that retirement community?"

The answer was curt: "*Just be!*"

I did not believe in "pennies from heaven," but on moving day, I found thirteen pennies, too many for chance alone. There were two outside of our house, one in the moving van, and one on each piece of furniture that the movers placed in my new apartment.

Moving required me to make many decisions about what to take and what to leave or throw away. One of the least significant things I considered was a bag of about twenty packages of Stim-U-Dents, which my husband had used to stimulate his gums. Because I had always been frugal, I decided to take them. After several weeks in my new home, I rediscovered the Stim-U-Dents. When I opened the little folder, there was President Abraham Lincoln's profile on a shiny new penny sitting atop of those little sticks. It was all the proof I needed to believe in pennies from heaven.

When the shock abated and I had added this penny to the others, which I now kept in a small purse, I began to wonder why my husband had chosen this way of getting my attention. After some thought, I realized that this was a perfect way. He was a shopaholic. Shopping temporarily lifted his chronic depression, but his excessive spending caused many arguments that sent him back into depression, requiring more spending. What a perfect way for a passive-aggressive shopaholic to show me, a penny-pincher, that he could now spend all the money he wishes to without hiding his purchases or arguing with me about them.

Foolish child, you thought this move was about freeing you from your responsibilities. It is about making you responsible for radiating the healing power of love throughout your community.

February 2001

I entered a deep, dark space without a thought and heard, *"Your work here has begun. Spread joy and love."*

Yesterday, when I noticed an open door and lots of activity in the apartment across the hall, I asked if I could come in. My neighbor had just returned from the hospital with a prognosis of "three months to live." While hospice personnel was scurrying about and setting up equipment, the patient told me that she was ready to die and that she could feel her deceased mother climbing into bed beside her. Guided by spirit, I do not remember what I shared, but my neighbor did not die in three months, but three years later. During those years, she was able to continue life as usual with some help. Had I been instructed to move to this community not only to "just be" but to heal, too?

Today, you blocked our guidance by your inability to handle the flow of energy we were sending. You are aware of a new life force, a new vitality flowing into you, but you haven't given it much thought. We need you to fulfill your commitment to us. The real work begins now. Be attentive. Everyone and everything is an opportunity to serve. We have been patiently waiting for this moment, and despite the fact that we have awakened you at about three o'clock in the morning for weeks, this is the first time you have been receptive to us.

Your job now is to gain control of your wandering mind, though not necessarily by meditating. You need to be in a meditative state all day long, so unless you need to think, don't. You can't be receptive to higher vibrations and soul-control unless your chattering mind is stopped. Even as you sleep, your mind chatters, but that is less of a problem. You are gaining some limited control of your impulsive nature. Practice being empty-headed as often as possible, day and night. Stop looking for things to occupy you. Time is of the essence. A quiet mind and body are of greater help to us than an active one. We find it easier to come early in the morning.

This is a critical period in human and planetary evolution. Humanity will take a leap in consciousness, infinitesimal according to our perspective but critical and huge from your perspective. We thank you for accepting our rather sudden directive to move despite the fact that we had previously told you not to move. It was the first step in freeing you from the need to occupy your time with trivia. Don't waste your precious freedom with the inconsequential. What you spend your time doing is less important than staying focused and aware of your self. Now is the time to fly, spiritually speaking. Don't cling to anyone in your past who is not taking flight as you are, and don't attach yourself emotionally to anyone as you have done in the past. Remember your need and desire to be free. When you travel, be aware of changes in vibration.

You ask about the book. As far as your big brothers and sisters are concerned, the book is not necessary, but it is important for your growth to complete what you started. Unfinished business is a drain on precious psychic energy. Guilt drains creativity. Stop spending so much time thinking about your physical being. It is your spirit that supports your life. Your physical problems will diminish as you focus on your relationship to us. While you are embodied, it will be impossible to be completely free of the physical and psychological consequences of being human. You chose a difficult incarnation in order to build your spiritual strength and to speed up the evolutionary process. Each of your choices, whether you consider them wrong or right, have taught you what you needed to learn.

March 2001

The energy/power is always available. Guard your thoughts carefully, allow no negatively to take hold, bless all silently, including yourself, have no expectations, and you will never be disappointed. Now you have the opportunity to grow to your fullness.

In the early nineteenth century, despondent over the loss of a child, I took one of my stockings, made a noose, slipped it over my head, and hanged myself from a beam in the cabin ceiling.

May 2001

Dear child of ours, we are fully aware of your struggles to overcome your weaknesses. You are being corrupted by the admiration of others. Beware! Humility is a virtue. We have chosen you to become enlightened and loving. Ego-building is unworthy of you. You are a transformer meant to bring more light and love into the world.

June 2001

Go beyond your self, stretch, not only by helping others but by being a spiritual example of loving compassion. In that state, your aura alone will raise others. When you feel like eating, focus on the change you are going through. You are being prepared for that quantum leap.

I'm expecting others to give me light, though I've been told that I'm the one most likely to be able to burn brightly. My masters have empowered me to change the world. That sounds very egotistical, but I say it with great humility and trepidation.

During this time of rebirthing, you need to be alone for longer periods of time than you have been taking for yourself. You've made the physical transition. Now it is time for a metaphysical transformation. You now need to become aware of your true multidimensional self. All that you are will be present at each moment, and you will be aware on more than one level. It is time to be born once again. Your purpose is written in your name. With each rebirth, you expand your consciousness. You need to expand your skills and to act in a more expansive way. You have been looking for us to guide you. Now it is time for you to realize that we are you and you are us. The words you write come from the reality where all is known.

The opening up of the individual into the cosmic consciousness is a necessary condition for the supramental change.[1]

I just wrote "Aegis" without knowing what it meant. The dictionary defined it as "a breastplate emblematic of majesty, patronage, sponsorship, protection and defense." Does this refer to the last initiation when the force of the "Rod of Initiation" was buffered so that I could accept it? (This esoteric reference can be found in the *Master Index of the Tibetan and Alice A. Bailey Books.)*

What Gerald Heard wrote about initiation is certainly true.

[Initiation is] a termination of ordinary life.[2]

The walls of Jericho are tumbling down, and you will soon realize that the level of spiritual achievement you once thought of as impossible, you are now approaching—a realm of unity, total reality. Realize that you have always been there. You are a shaman with access to everything and anything.

You are without boundaries, without limitations, intellectual, physical, and spiritual. Your mind, body, and spirit are at last free. You are transformed.

We are not temporal, but because we believe in time and space, we are bounded by them. If I was bound by time, how could I know the future or the past? If I was bound by space, how could I have left my body so many times? To remain outside of the worldly belief and inside the universal truth is to be in the real world.

Consciousness has to rid itself of its involvement with past and future.[3]

November 2001

Although I had never sounded my small chime before meditation, I struck it three times this morning. A burst of energy encircled my chest at the level of the heart and slowly moved to my neck and shoulders. The pain of several months was gone. I awaited a message that I intuitively knew was coming:

> *You've had a healing, but don't put any unnecessary strain on your neck and shoulders. No sitting up in bed to watch TV, no reading in bed. You will need to sit at your computer for several hours a day to write. Perhaps you should title the book* The Autobiography of a Mystic *or* Journals of a Mystic. *Remember when you asked us what you were to do in your community? We said, "Just be." All is being. By being you can realize your power, God power. Nothing else is real. You are here as love. Your power is your ability to express love. Remember that, and stop focusing on unreality, what you have been conditioned to give your power to, such as food, appearance, pain, illness. Stop filling yourself with your imagined needs. You already have power, beauty, love, health, and life eternal. Any change must take place in*

consciousness before it is manifested.

We must free ourselves from human bondage as well as all of the beliefs that we have about this world, others, and ourselves.

Some time ago, you looked into a mirror and saw yourself as you really are, a soul in a temporary body. You cried and wished to be released from that body, but it is not time for you to go yet.

These periods of greater awareness, which come in flashes, especially when you remove yourself from the hubbub of activity, will increase. You need more time alone. Your healing powers will increase. They aren't exactly your powers but the powers of the universe. You will be able to heal yourself once this evolutionary process reaches its perigee, the closest point to the center of power. Your trip to South Africa was needed to put you in touch with your love of nature. Tune in consciously to all aspects of nature. Pick a flower or a leaf every day. Put it in the bedroom with the starfish and the crystal. Go out at night and look at the stars. Sirius, the brightest star, is part of your constellation Taurus. Mineral, animal, plant, human, and celestial are all connection points. I know it all seems strange and incomprehensible to you now, but you will soon realize its significance. Your trip to South America will not be as spiritually significant as your trip to Ireland will be.

This was the strangest message. The reference to Sirius and the word "perigee" was definitely incomprehensible to me. I did not plan to go to South America or Ireland, although I had sometimes thought about going to both places.

I wondered why I needed so much suffering in this incarnation. Was it necessary to evolve more quickly?

You no longer need pain to grow. You are now able to consciously evolve and transform. Now you know immediately when you are transgressing or acting without awareness. While you are in a physical body, you are never completely pure, but you are pure enough to help others, without envy, resentment, or expectations.

The people you are drawing to you are mirrors in which you see your own reflection.

Chapter Twenty-Three
Thoughts about Sex

December 2001

> Women need a reason to have sex. Men need a place.
> Billy Crystal

> Sex is not apart from or against Spirit, but is
> simply the lowest or most fundamental of Spirit's
> expressions, and so a person's sexual nature is one of
> the easiest of the many threads that can be used to
> return to Spirit.[1]

I am pondering the mystery of sex. There are animals and plants that are hermaphroditic and some reef fish that can change their sex from male to female or female to male. How does having different sexes advance evolution in the case of human beings? Could it be that two different natures and two different forms of consciousness are needed for balance? Our brains have two hemispheres. Each has a different function, but they also must work together.

Sexual intercourse can lead to an experience of transcendence, but it is certainly not the only path to transcendence. We all have had at least one transcendent experience. It may have been while looking at the stars, the ocean, or an exceptional work of art. It may have occurred while we were listening to a beautiful piece of music, or it may have been while we were making love. When lovers are focused on sensation, transcendent experiences are blocked. Most of our lives are spent absorbed in the past or the future, but during sexual intercourse, we are not thinking of the past or the future. We are in the moment.

> It is when interest is completely engrossed in an
> experience outside the sensory self that consciousness
> is most alive.[2]

Animals are compelled by necessity to reproduce, but what makes sexual intercourse so compelling for us humans? It can be a moment of complete surrender, a moment of oblivion, a moment of giving oneself to another. During climax, a man gives many potential selves in his ejaculate. A woman literally loses body boundaries when she opens to a man. Thus, her surrender is extended beyond the climax.

When man and woman come together, if ego is shattered, the potential for a spiritual union is realized, and it can be the beginning of a new life for both.

> Whenever two are linked in this way, there comes
> another from the unseen world. It may be through
> birth, if nothing prevents conception, but a third does
> come, when two unite in love, or in hate. The intense
> qualities born of such joining appear in the spiritual
> world.[3]

The first time I had sexual intercourse with the man who was to become my second husband, there was no lovemaking, nothing but sex, or so I thought. I don't remember many of the particulars, but the experience of total surrender was unique. It was mystical. As our bodies interlaced, we became one, not metaphorically but spiritually. Instantly and magically, we were sure that God had brought us together and had a plan for us. This remarkable sense of a spiritual destiny made our love powerful and sealed our fates. That belief kept us together for forty-one years until his death. We became Romeo and Juliet, willing to die rather than be separated.

I was twenty-five years old, separated from my husband, and I had a five-year-old daughter. Because I needed a job, I began looking in the want ads. The want ad I answered read, "Wanted: private secretary for chief engineer of manufacturing company." It was a bold or rather desperate move to apply for that job, because I had not used shorthand or typing since high school. Nevertheless, I was interviewed and hired by the operations manager, because my boss-to-be was unavailable.

Why I should still have such a vivid memory of our first brief meeting is strange, because there were many other significant moments in my life that I don't remember with such vividness.

It was Wednesday, December 5, 1951, at about ten o'clock in the morning, and I was being inducted into the telephone switchboard operator's relief system. She was putting me through my paces on that confounding contraption known as the now-defunct manual switchboard when he walked into the office. My instructor stopped him and said, "Mr. Krushel, I would like to introduce you to your new secretary, Mrs. F."

He looked at me and said, "How do you do?" in rather cold acknowledgment before he moved on. Although his eyes showed no warmth and he did not even smile, I saw my future. I would one day be his wife. It was the first of many ineffable experiences that were to come. I later learned that he was married and that his wife had just delivered their third child, the first boy.

What about love makes us dare all and break with what is socially acceptable and in accord with our own morality? How can one love so much that nothing else matters? Is it more than mad passion that drives one to break all social morals? Joseph Campbell emphatically stated that the love not sanctioned by society, the love you will die for, is the highest form of love.

Rumi understood the ineffability of love.

> Advice doesn't help lovers!
> They're not the kind of mountain stream
> you can build a dam across.

> An intellectual doesn't know
> what the drunk is feeling!

Don't try to figure
what those lost in love
will do next![4]

This is a poem I wrote:

When I fell in love,
You became the lesser god I worshipped.
I quivered when you touched me.
Your kisses made me like butter.
Whenever you called, I came.
I could not resist.
When first our bodies joined,
My surrender was more than physical.
It was spiritual.
We were united forever by God.

In Eastern traditions, the surrendering of oneself in sexual union represents the surrendering of the self to God. In the *Bhagavad Gita*, Krishna tells Arjuna that surrender is the easiest way to self-transcendence. The total loss of self as it merges with God is the final goal of the spiritual life.

The abundance of sexual intercourse images in Hinduism is not meant to be erotic but to symbolize that duality ceases to exist when lovers unite. The yin and yang as well as the lingam and yoni are ancient symbols of male and female energies, two aspects of the same reality. Sexual union is a prelude to the union with God. According to my glimpse into the future while I was riding on a bus in Australia, we won't need sex to demonstrate that unity. We will know it. There will be loving unions between groups of people without sex.

Andrew Cohen links sexual passion with the passion to evolve, and Barbara Marx Hubbard speaks of a supra-sexual co-creation as a means of creating a new humanity. Have Cohen and Hubbard intuited a transformation from the urge to reproduce, to the passionate urge to create new forms of consciousness? I think so.

To become one with another is to die to oneself, to

be divided by the entrance of another into oneself; to love is to be penetrated or inhabited by the other.[5]

The human being possesses himself by giving himself; this is the essential mystery of love.[6]

Surrender is the easiest way to self-transcendence.[7]

Once the heart is opened by love, it must remain open for spiritual growth to continue. However, often when the romance is over and the lover is no longer a God substitute, disillusion sets in. Then anger, blame, and disappointment close the heart. When they say love is blind, it is true in one sense—the beloved is often seen as perfect. Is the mystic able to maintain the belief in the image of perfection longer than a nonmystic? Or does the mystic see the spirit's perfection?

Andrew Cohen sees the sexual impulse as evolutionary.

The drive to procreate is the physical expression of the evolutionary impulse. The same creative urge that propelled something to burst out of nothing fourteen billion years ago.[8]

These thoughts about sex are cursory. If you would like to further investigate this very complex subject, I suggest Ken Wilber's *Sex, Ecology, Spirituality: The Spirit of Evolution.*

Chapter Twenty-Four
Romania

When you cease to make a contribution you begin to
die. Eleanor Roosevelt

June 2002

Now that I was settled in my new community and the desire to do
something for others was growing, I decided to continue the volunteer
work I had been doing from time to time since 1952.

While looking through a Global Volunteers brochure for
opportunities, I was halted by a picture of an older woman holding
two babies while being surrounded by others who had no one to hold
them. Instantly, I decided that she needed help and was going to get
it. In a few days, I will be leaving for Romania to give loving care
and attention to failure to thrive infants, many of whom have been
abandoned by their parents.

Last night. I received a parting message:

*So glad you recognized our presence. Your
trip to Romania will be successful from our point
of view—that is, it will serve the plan to have you
in Romania. Whatever happens in the hospital*

or the school from your or another's perspective is insignificant compared to what your presence there will mean to us. Be assured that we are with you wherever you are. While you are in that country, we will be flooding you with love and light. Keep us in mind as much as possible. You will be a catalyst for change in consciousness on a grander scale than you can imagine. We are pleased that you chose this assignment with your heart rather than your head.

Keep positive no matter what happens. Send love to all you encounter, especially the babies. You are going as our ambassador. We will sustain you physically and spiritually and will keep you in our hearts. Have no doubt about your effectiveness. We guarantee it. You are more than a good will ambassador; you are a living-light ambassador. Thank you for following your heart. We love you and will be with you always. Bon voyage!

July 2002

I went to Romania intending to help with failure to thrive infants, but someone had to teach English in a middle school for two weeks. Because none of the other volunteers were willing to accept the assignment, I did. The youngsters and I had lots of fun, and I presume they learned some English. After that assignment, there was only one week with the babies. I was registered for three weeks, the maximum for that location.

There were thirty children, four or five were toddlers, and the rest were infants. The conditions at the so-called hospital were miserable, though they have improved since then with the financial help of volunteers and others.

Nicu, an autistic baby boy, did not relate to anything or anyone. In the infant room, while the other babies were crawling over one another like ants investigating their environment, Nicu was totally absorbed by the mobile that hung above his head and protected him from most contacts. In an effort to get him to relate to others, I tried many things with some success. On my last day, with Nicu in a stroller, we took a walk around the hospital grounds. When I stooped to tickle his nose with a flower that I had just picked, he fixed his wise, all-knowing eyes on my eyes for several seconds. During those few seconds, we did not exist as separate beings. All boundaries had dissolved. We had become one. This was a mystical moment as profound as any I had ever experienced, and even though it seemed to last for only a few seconds, it lasted for an eternity at a different level of reality.

Leaving Nicu broke my heart, but I had to go. Since then, I have made several attempts to find out how he is doing, but strangely, nobody remembers Nicu. I will never forget him.

We are glad that you responded to our vibration so quickly. Don't worry about your cough. Fear is debilitating. The impact you had on the lives of the children of Romania is profound in ways you cannot understand. Continue to live intuitively and respond to our input. We know that life on your planet is very difficult, especially for our disciples. Living in two worlds requires great balance. "Balance" is a word you have received many times, and you are well aware of its significance in your life as you attempt to fulfill your mundane and spiritual obligations. You are on a lonely journey. Pay more attention to your higher impulses, if we can call them that, rather than the ego impulses you have a habit of responding to. Your awareness of our oneness is dawning. If it helps you to address yourself to us through the great sage Ramana Maharshi, continue to do so, but be aware of the overriding unity of all.

We know it is natural for you to feel closer to some individuals, but remember to avoid personal attachments that will allow negativity to enter. We need you free from personal entanglements that might disrupt our transmissions. We love and protect you, but we need you to cooperate now that your understanding has grown. Love and light be with you.

Chapter Twenty-Five
Renunciation

The mystic … has been called a lonely soul. He might more properly be described as a lonely body; for his soul, peculiarly responsive, sends out and receives communications upon every side.[1]

July 2002

The sainthood you desire again awaits you. Your two saintly masters await you. Time is relative. Now you see yourself as very far from the goal, but a quantum leap will bring you to your goal before you can imagine. I know that's hard to believe. Have faith, which doesn't require belief. Stop dwelling on your unworthiness. What your body is enduring is of little consequence as long as you realize that it is not the real you.

The gravity of the earth must be escaped. This gravity consists of everything that is dark and heavy—fear, doubt, negativity, disease, ego gratification of all kinds. See yourself escaping from the pull of the earth and all attachments. Clear the way for yourself by overcoming everything that stands in your way.

A person who has not become transparent, that is, who is not yet his essential self, is like a diamond, embedded in a rock. We are all beings of light, but we must chip away the nonessentials.

While in the grips of craving sweets, I rationalize by saying that as a child I didn't get enough sweets or that I'm still at the Freudian stage of oral fixation. Knowing all the reasons doesn't help. Gluttony is the desire for more than you need. Aurobindo suggests that choosing a beautiful form is a higher good than eating to please the senses. Edgar Cayce's fearsome prophesy proclaims that gratifying the senses closes the door to spiritual life. That scares me, because there is nothing more important to me than my spiritual life. When you eat to gratify senses, you lower your vibration.

To consume what you like rather than what your body needs for health is madness. You treat the body as an "it" instead of a "thou." Our bodies are on loan to us for a very short time. When we contaminate them, we contaminate the earth where they will lie and decay after we depart.

Do you remember when I told you that you have no idea of the blessing you will receive when you are no longer attached to food? Stop focusing on what's wrong. Focus on what's right. Create your own happiness. See yourself as a butterfly breaking out of a cocoon and flying free from the imprisonment of the past with its obsessions and desires. The gravity of the earth must be escaped. You see yourself as very far from the goal. A quantum leap is timeless and spaceless. I know that is hard to believe. Don't believe it. Have faith. What you are enduring is of little consequence as long as you realize that it is not the real you. Clear away everything that stands in your way. Every fearful or negative thought must be released, not buried. Free yourself from ego identity. Your masters await you.

August 2002

We are glad you decided to return to daily meditation. You are having difficulties because you are not centering your life on us, your other self, so to speak. Stop drifting in an ocean of petty, unresolved problems. Do something purposeful every day. Yesterday, you helped E. M. That was a good, selfless act, but then you spent the rest of the day lying around and worrying. You need more focus and discipline. Every day, decide to do something that needs doing. Undertake one project a day. Organize your physical environment, because it keeps your mind positive. You've been wasting precious time for the past six weeks, thinking about your problems. You waste time, and then you punish yourself—that is more wasted time and energy.

Stop participating in gossip and small talk.

How can I master my ego's lethargy, worries, and desires? It is painful to be so aware of one's faults. I have been directed to review my journals.

Truth is available to all but must be earned.
Life is not to be wasted. It must be purposeful.

Lack of discipline, attachments, desires, and impulses are running my life, postponing wisdom.

Gurdjieff says of attachments:

Only when an individual is ready to give up his most intimate attachments is he free to receive something indescribably glorious.[2]

Last night, I asked for healing. My hands grew very hot. I sent the heat into my aching body, and this morning, I am well.

October 2002

An impulse is a false identification with thought. Adverse forces can be distinguished by their suddenness and their vibration. They discourage the seeker. The moment a thought enters the mind, examine it for its usefulness.

Once again, I'm not burning when I touch hot things.

I am appalled by my lack of direction and my preoccupation with physical problems.

At 5:30 AM, I went into the kitchen for something to eat but returned to the bedroom without the food, because my physical body was becoming a phantom; I was only aware of the subtle bodies and consciousness.

With a greater awareness of my body developing, I know it requires loving care.

> *Treat the body as you would the body of Christ. It no longer belongs to you. Have only creative and loving thoughts. Guard against any form of negativity.*
>
> *Every message from us is important, be it one word like "balance" or one letter like the "U" in AUM.*

November 2002

It is 2:22 AM, emptied of thought, knowing nothing, aware only of the dark emptiness—no light yet. I am in shock, frightened by the unknown. I take a breath and quake from head to toe. Just born, alone in a strange new world, an unknown world, without a guide or companion, there is no one that can share this world. Like an amoeba feeling around for something recognizable and finding nothing I was alone. Everything that was familiar is cold and dead. "In the valley of the shadow of death, I will fear no evil." In this dark and foreboding realm barred to most, inhabited by dragons and menacing guardians waiting to eject me, I am a trespasser. "Do not be frightened!" Part of me thinks of grounding myself with the familiar—food, TV, anything that will bring me back to the known. But I will not retreat. I will not budge. I will stay with my fear.

Early this morning, I died to the flesh and was born to the spirit. I am at a juncture where the masters and I may become one in consciousness. The discipline necessary to remain aware is critical and expected. When the inner master takes over, you are free to realize your unity with all ascended masters. I remember that Master Ramana Maharshi taught me: "We are all one." For the first time, I realize that I can no longer utter prayers or make requests of a master. The master is me. Like the young tiger who thought he was a lamb until he saw his face, I awoke this morning to my own true identity.

Forgive me. I would like to clarify things, but my experiences are otherworldly. They can't be explained rationally, and even I don't fully understand them.

During meditation, when I begin to think of the masters as separate entities, something immediately blocks the sense of separateness and reaffirms unity.

Yesterday's experience was forecast by the masters in June of 2001. At that time, the message about rebirthing was totally incomprehensible. It still is, even though I have experienced it.

The Chinese Master told me that I was being prepared for the fourth initiation. My move to the retirement community was the first step. It required giving up many things. The fourth initiation is the crucifixion, which requires giving up the self. I gave up my former life to serve in my retirement community. I hope this was the first step toward the fourth initiation, which the Chinese Master thought might take another incarnation.

January 2003

I intuit that God's agents, angels, guides, and masters are attempting to purify me. Is the quaking an acknowledgment? Things that weaken me are being withdrawn, and I am coming closer to becoming my true self. An affirmative shaking happens. (By an affirmative shaking, I mean that my body shakes or vibrates after some experience to indicate the correctness of my interpretation.) The caterpillar has been satiated and is withdrawing into its cocoon. What will emerge I don't know. Once, I emerged as a white butterfly.

I see a six-pointed star. As the ascendant triangle longs for the descendent, the descendent responds by penetrating the ascendant, creating a new being, a six-pointed star. It has a single-pointed bottom and a single-pointed top, thus, it represents unity. The five-pointed star does not complete the descent of the spirit. The top has three points representing trinity, but the bottom has two. Two is duality. Did this idea come from the six-pointed star I saw or from another source?

Figure 2

A child represents the union of opposites. It is non-dual until made conscious of duality by society.

My paintings of paths that show beginnings but no endings, doorways, and other entrances and exits, symbolize the mystery of life, the road without end, the mobius strip, and the figure eight, the infinity symbol.

As I approach the end of another cycle, another phase of renunciation, I am giving up my membership in the Women's Club, membership in three art associations, and wonder of wonders. I am giving my car to my daughter.

As usual, I was awakened at 3:33 AM. Three times three is the number of perfected man and the number of the goddess, according to Joseph Campbell. It is my number and the number of the mathematical equation given to me years ago.

February 2003

My spirit is calling me to renounce the world. What is going on? Am I on a seesaw that is on a merry-go-round? Am I up and down and round and round, never progressing, or am I making my way to the center of the labyrinth like Theseus, holding tight to Ariadne's golden thread, which will take me back to who I was before I was born?

March 2003

A pinkish violet vibrant field obscured my reflection as I looked into the mirror. What was that? No explanation followed.

April 2003

When will my attachment to sweets end?

May 2003

It is 10:00 PM. I am losing awareness of my physical body.

As I read, the words become highlighted in gold. That hasn't happened for many years. Does it mean that despite my confusion, I am filled with light?

When am I going to be free of the ego? The higher mind must control the body's energy system. Desire is the cause of all suffering.

For the past few days, I have felt a presence around me, and I have seen fleeting shadows.

When things do not happen as planned, I no longer react negatively. For example, when the trip to Master Sri Ramana Maharshi's ashram was cancelled, I accepted it with only the slightest disappointment, devoid of emotion. Pleased by my ability to accept the disappointment without an emotional charge, Master R. M. compassionately promised, "*You don't have to come to me, I will come to you.*"

> The real proof of one's progress on the spiritual path can be realized by how indifferent one is to every situation in life. **Indifference and independence** are the two wings that enable the soul to fly.[3]

October 2003

This evening, for no apparent reason, years of self-doubt washed away, and I was hanging out in space, infused with the confidence of the sun. How it happened I don't know, but as the sun brought forth new life, it spawned a belief that I was creative in a limitless way, totally godlike.

November 2003

During another dark night of the soul, I wanted to escape the pain of feeling alone, the profusion and confusion of mystical experiences, the pain of believing that I had been deserted by the very beings that once graced me, and the pain of feeling inadequate.

It was only a month ago that I realized I had godlike creativity. When you are climbing Jacob's ladder, you never know what will be on the next rung.

David Hawkins relates some of the discomforts of a mystic.[4]

December 2003

I feel entrained by my master. My head is hot. My body is vibrating, and I receive this message:

> *Transcend your present level of conscious-ness. You are manifesting these problems by your belief in limitation, pain, and weakness. Your belief in some magic pill (Echinacea) is al-lowing for the cure, not the pill itself. Work on those erroneous beliefs about everything that seems wrong. You are sustaining the symptoms by your belief.*

November 2004

When I spoke of love while I was visiting a friend in the hospital, the words created their own powerful energy field, which enveloped and healed us both.

Chapter Twenty-Six
Travels

May 2005

In Chile, as soon as I stepped off the tour bus and approached the courtyard of the church once attended by Gabriela Mistral, Chile's Nobel Laureate, a very unique energy shrouded me. Because I wanted to be alone, I sat on a bench outside while the rest of the group entered the church. Unfortunately a conversing couple sat beside me, disrupting the energy.

At seventy-nine, because I have already let go of the nonessentials in my life, I am focused on perfecting myself in order to become a more perfect instrument for transmitting love, light, and healing.

As Henry Miller says:

One's destination is never a place, but a new way of seeing things.

In another past life regression I saw myself in the ashram of my Master R. M., scurrying about attending to chores.

August 2005

I am Taurus the bull, and as Joseph Campbell claims the bull is killed to be resurrected. At least once every seven years, I experience death and resurrection. When I was forty-nine (seven times seven), I experienced a profound sense of dying to my former self. For the ancient Greeks, every seven years represented a major change in life.

> To exist is to change; to change is to mature; to mature is to go on creating oneself endlessly. Henri Bergson

September 2005

On a trip to Ireland that was advertised as a "Women's Spiritual Journey." I became vividly aware of my fiery connection to Mother Earth.

> The "fire in the head" refers to *imbas,* an old Irish term for the state of inspiration or heightened consciousness.[1]

We visited many secluded stone circles created and used thousands of years ago for pagan ceremonies. Two guardian boulders stood at the entrance to one of the stone circles. Though I presumed that all rocks felt the same, I decided to touch each boulder. They were not the same. The boulder on the right felt strong and aggressive, but the one on the left felt weak and recessive. When I shared my experience with our tour guide, she stated matter-of-factly, "One is feminine, the other masculine." I should have asked her which was feminine, because thousands of years ago, the goddesses had been the strong, aggressive ones.

In a large park, we met with a "tree person" who walked around naming trees and giving us their symbolic significance. Tired by now, when we were asked to stand against a tree, I stood against the nearest tree. While we meditated, I saw a very graphic image of a forest that had been devastated by fire. Astounded by the image, I shared it with the tree man, who asked me to show him which tree I had chosen. Shocked is hardly a word strong enough to describe my reaction to what he told me. I had been shown a memory snapshot by the one tree in that area most vulnerable to fire.

Next, we were told to pick up any stick. This time, I was more selective. As I ambled about, I waited for a stick to ask to be picked. Told that I had chosen a twig from the most holy and powerful of trees, the elder, pleased me. After some shamanic drumming, piping, and rattling, we were asked to pick a rune. I chose "Sumerian goddess," the most powerful and loved of all the goddesses. How was it that I had picked the most powerful tree and the most powerful goddess—coincidence or synchronicity?

At Knowth, we entered one of the Megalithic passage tombs. The energy in that ancient stone-domed room overpowered me, and I had to take hold of our leader's arm to keep from collapsing. Thereafter, she kept me at some distance from places that she considered too powerful for me. My receptivity to earth energies was a complete surprise.

We continued touring. At one stop, we visited a healer who took us to a nearby field to meditate. She sat next to me, and in a quiet but firm voice, she declared, "You are a healer!"

Several times during our tour of Ireland, a clairvoyant member of our group confronted me by saying, "You are blocking something!" She would not say what it was, but because we were on a spiritual journey, I assumed it had something to do with my spiritual evolution.

Back home, I thought about being blocked. Was I blocking the writing of this book? Was I blocking accepting myself as a mystic? Was I blocking accepting myself as a healer? Yes, I was blocking all three, because they frightened me. Long ago, I gave up any thought of healing after two huge failures, both against cancer—one had been a teacher, and the other had been my husband. I had hidden my mysticism and had not yet committed myself completely to writing the book. If I was a healer, why hadn't my masters told me so? While I was going back over my journals, I discovered that on March 2, 1983, my master had told me that I would be channeling healing energy and would learn to heal myself and others.

You do not love and accept yourself. You talk much and practice little the things you have been graced to experience. It is all about living the enlightenment, not thinking and talking about it.

October 2005

Muladhara, the base chakra, was on fire this morning. Fortunately, the energy moved up through all the chakras, exploding out of the top of my head, my toes, my fingers, and once again, I had a healing.

March 2006

> *Correct yourself without condemning yourself. You were Saint Catherine of Siena. Wake up to who you are.*

I feel guilty for not trusting the words of my masters, but I can't believe that I was Saint Catherine of Siena. How could I have become less than I once was? If I was Catherine I have to strive to reach my utmost potential during this very difficult incarnation.

In 1979, during what seemed like a vivid dream, I was ordained and wrapped in a red cloak. Was that a memory of Saint Catherine of Siena? She was canonized in 1461 by Pope Pius XI and proclaimed doctor of the church in 1970. We shared the mystical marriage and many other less spectacular mystical experiences.

> *Take your life seriously. Stop dawdling, fritting away hours. Stop denying who you are and manifest spirit. Why do you keep belittling yourself? I've opened you up. Reveal your true self, not to others but to yourself. What you have feared is upon you. You have a responsibility. I will direct you. Pay attention.*
>
> *Overcome your fears and reveal yourself. The time has come. In the thirteenth and fourteenth*

century, the mystics were often sainted. That was even more frightening than persecution. How many of you have the courage to come forward? Reveal your hidden voices, miracles, visions, and messages. The time has come to tell the world about mystic revelations.

Mystics are often more guarded than homosexuals. They fear scorn and rejection. I have hidden my mysticism from almost all of my acquaintances, friends, and family. However, recently, on the advice of my masters and a couple of psychics whom I met in Ireland, I decided to reveal myself, to come out from behind the veil of ego.

The soul's journey toward enlightenment requires courage. It takes one into visionary realms. The guardians on the threshold are frightening. They are the parts of your ego self trying to keep you from finding out who you really are.

June 2006

Impulsive and undisciplined, I have tried using schedules and lists to keep me on task, but it never seems to work. Much of my exuberant creative energy is wasted rearranging things in the apartment. I need to stay focused on important things rather than scattering precious energy, which I can not afford to do at my age.

I decided to spend a week at a Tibetan Buddhist retreat.

Thrilled by the multitude of colorful images in the meditation hall, I wandered about, wondering if I could feel vibrations. As I moved from idol to icon, although I did not know who she was, beautiful Green Tara stopped me. Her emanation was penetrating. As I continued past a row of golden Buddhas, I felt nothing. However, at the end of the hall, I again felt radiations coming from a male statue. Like Tara, he also was a bodhisattva. Maybe it wasn't strange but appropriate, because I had often wondered if I might be a bodhisattva, having committed myself to reincarnation until all of humanity has been enlightened and liberated.

Before I left the retreat center, I purchased a small statue of Green Tara, who now sits beside a brass Buddha in my bedroom. At home, I asked Tara what my purpose for this incarnation was. She replied, "*We are needed for healing and wholeness.*"

Why had she used "we?" She could have said, "You are needed for healing and wholeness." Was she including me in the category of bodhisattva?

August 2006

Finally, you are recognizing the magic of your life. We, your guides, have been trying to attract your attention for years, but you have been so focused on your recognized masters that you haven't noticed us. We have been guiding you since before you were born. You have guides and angels who would appreciate your recognition and love. Our names are not important. You have gone beyond the emotional and the mystical, and you are now ready for superhuman evolution. Your mind is expanding, and previously dormant parts of your brain are awakening. Where it will lead depends on your cooperation and your sensitivity to our direction. Stop focusing on what you think are physical and mental limitations. Become pure and fearless.

Could this superhuman evolution that the master just spoke of be what Aurobindo wrote about in the following?

> For our **humanity is not the whole of Reality or its best possible self-formation or self-expression**—the Reality as assumed before man existed an infrahuman formation and self-creation and can assume after him or in him a superhuman formation and self-creation.[2]

Once again, the top of my head is taking the form of a satellite dish. Will I become more receptive to incoming communications? If not, why is it happening? There I go, trying to understand what cannot be understood by the intellect.

September 2006

How heartbreaking it is to spend our lives looking for love without recognizing that we are already loved by God, masters, guides, angels, and our own spirit. We seek the conditional love of humans, not knowing that we are continually bathed in unconditional love. If we would give every cell in our body unconditioned love, think of what we might become. While I was contemplating these things, I picked up a book to read, and to my astonishment, a golden light highlighted the words. But as soon as I objectified the light by thinking and naming it, it was gone.

> The mental process must give place to an inward mystical perception that is not thinking, but knowing.[3]

There is a difference between emotions and feelings. Feelings are below the level of the mind. Emotions are our interpretations of feelings. When we have a strong feeling that we interpret as a threat, we react with a primitive "fight or flight" response, using only past experiences already clouded by past interpretations. If we can stay with the feeling and allow it to reveal its root cause, we will grow in self-awareness.

For example, my husband, mystified by my mysticism years ago, asked, "Who are you?"

Though unbecoming of a mystic, I flew into a rage, but unlike other times when my rage might have reached hysterical proportion and escalated to a perceived attack, I went off by myself this time and stayed with the feeling. My willingness to stay with the feeling resulted in a profound healing. I allowed the feeling to reveal itself. What it revealed was a confused, abandoned child who had never known who she was or to whom she belonged. Forgotten or repressed images flashed before me: relatives with whom I had lived, strangers asking me who I was and where my mother and father were. When the images stopped, a lonely, sad, and confused little girl surfaced. I told her that she belonged to me, that I loved her very much, and that I would give her the nurturing and love she never had. Not in my wildest dream could I ever have imagined what staying with my feeling would have revealed. Since then, I have used feelings instead of emotions to grow in self-awareness and to heal myself. Most people believe the thoughts that are based on their emotions and are afraid of their feelings.

October 2006

Though I thought that my masters, guides, and angels had never directly told me I was a healer, a strong vibration woke me at 2:22 AM, and I heard, "*A transformer of energy is a healer.*" For me, this message verified that someone knew what I was thinking at all times. As a transformer of energy, I didn't take an active part in the healing.

February 2007

As I have mentioned, my paintings show threshold images. According the Celtic tradition, May 1st, my birthday, is one of the important thresholds or gates to the "Otherworld."

> **Thresholds** are not the place of life and not the place
> of death. In their narrow confines you may find
> fantasy, memory, dreams, anxiety, miracle, intuition,

and magic. These are the means by which deep soul prospers—neither in life nor entirely out of life ... **It is the true home of creativity.**[4]

May 2007

As I considered another spiritual trip, I chose a trip to Sedona Arizona. The trip was to be led by a shaman. Despite the fact that my arthritis was bothering me, I managed to climb those rocky red peaks in order to meditate at places of power. Though I had no expectations, I was surprised to feel the powerful energies. During drum-beating, rattle-shaking, and smoke rituals, I saw perhaps as many as twenty American-Indian faces and heard, "Hallowed burning ground, and scarcity." Was I developing a new psychic ability? In Ireland, two boulders indicated their sex. A tree revealed its history, and now Indians long gone from this place appeared and dropped four words into my consciousness.

Chapter Twenty-Seven
Revelation

June 2007

*This is an initiatory period for you. Your masters
are attending. Continue what you are teaching
and learning. This is the time of your awakening
to us. We need you to become more sensitive to
our presence. When you think about your body
and its pains and desires, you block us.*

As I stood looking at Master Maharshi's picture on my dresser, I
heard him say, *"You are a healer."* He obviously knew that I had
written or thought, "None of my masters have told me that I was a
healer." I thanked him for his kind assurance.

*Stop identifying with your physical body. Start
focusing on the luminous field that you are now
sensing. Don't look back. Reject all thoughts
and habits of the past. When you focus on
any negativity, past or present, you block your
awakening. Stop claiming humanity's negativity*

as your own. Do whatever is necessary to clear your mind so that it is free to soar to other dimensions. We are attending your rebirth. You have X number of years to perfect yourself. You are here to take your place in the transformation of humanity.

They named the number of years, but I choose not to reveal it here.

August 2007

Awakened at 3:00 AM by a strong vibration, I had the impression that I was being healed. At 7:00 AM, while I was putting on my makeup, I noticed that the suspicious spot on my cheek, a potential basil cell carcinoma, was gone.

September 2007

When I read in *Mother Theresa's Agony* that she had spent fifty years in a depressed state, yearning to feel at one with Jesus, a profound sadness shamed me. How could it have been that such a magnificent woman had suffered as a result of feeling abandoned by Jesus and God while I have been blessed by the love of many masters, including Jesus?

October 2007

During a very brief spontaneous regression, I saw myself as a nun in a closet-sized room reading the Bible by candlelight. Was this a third incarnation as a nun or a snapshot of one of the previous two? It really didn't matter.

Don't teach those who are not ready. Teach

by example. You are responsible for the negative reaction that you provoke when you try to change people. Good is an anathema to those who harbor evil. They will react to truth and good negatively. What you focus on receives your power, so don't focus on what you don't want. By judging or condemning others, you are judging and condemning yourself, because we are all one. Take no pride in your spiritual accomplishments. The mind records multisensory perceptions of continual present moments. It has a record of everything that was or will be.

May 2008

"Review your journals!," my master said.

Each time I hear this, I obey and subsequently find something that I have forgotten, something they, guides or masters, require me to remember. Today, it was the declaration that an impulse is a false identification with thought. Each thought has a vibration, and it should be evaluated before acceptance or rejection.

My spirit is projecting a small center of consciousness called the physical body in order to experience this plane of existence.

"Cast a rune," said someone..

When I heard this, I looked for the bag of runes but couldn't find it. I was then told to open the rune book to any page. I opened to Dagaz, meaning breakthrough or transformation. A voice interpreted the rune:

The book has to be written now. Don't think of failure. Hard work will be necessary, but we, your guides, will help. We need your intellect, your light, and your love. You must bring lower vehicles into accord with spirit. You must discriminate between ego impulses and Monad promptings. When a thought arises, wait and check its motivation and purpose. Ask, "Will this enhance ego or Monad control?" Kundalini can reverse the aging process. You are an evolutionary prototype.

Me? An evolutionary prototype?

When he describes an individual who experiences cosmic consciousness, Richard Bucke says, "he is almost a member of a **new species**."[1]

There is a greater purpose than you can realize to everything that happens in your life.

June 2008

As my masters directed, I was able to displace a strong sense of unworthiness with a strong sense of gratitude. This incarnation is just a moment in the life of spirit. If focus creates reality as quantum physics tells us, we must be very careful about what we focus on.

During a lecture, Dean Radin explained, "when we delve into matter everything we know about the world dissolves and there is no time, no space, only information and connectivity. It is the experience of all mystics."[2]

Time and time again, the masters have drilled, "Love yourself as we love you," but by now, you well know that I find it difficult to accept myself.

Negative thoughts and emotions block the flow of energy, but socialization and the habits of a lifetime are hard to remove.

August 2008

While he was instructing me, Master R. M. used a metaphor to show me how Reality with a capital "R" differed from reality with a small "r," the commonly shared reality on our planet. Our reality is but an image projected onto the screen of space and time.

Andrew Cohen and Ken Wilber came close to explaining my evolving concept of God. In their conversations called *The Three Faces of God*, Wilber used grammatical terms, such as first person, second person, and third person, to define the three aspects of God. God as first person is the "I Am" represented by an experience of being at one with everything that is. God as second person is the "Thou," the divine to whom we bow, a personal God. God as third person is creator, the totality of all that is.[3]

I experienced the first face of God as the one without the other in 1972 during what I call my Samadhi or enlightenment. There was no me, no other, only consciousness. I experienced the second face of God as the one to whom I had dedicated my life. I experienced the third face of God as the creator whose creation is continually evolving, the God who needs me to become co-creative.

September, 2008

What you hear comes from us. We are always aware of your comings and your goings. We understand your confusion. There are many of us, and we have different ways of speaking. You ask what you are to do in the time you have left. You are to come to terms with your ego and stop the conflict between it and your soul. You are to become one, undivided, without conflict. The energies of the body are in conflict with each other. As long as you are divided, you cannot be fully of service.

Eat when you are hungry. Don't listen to the false voices locked in your subconscious, some from other incarnations. Listen to the nature body, not to the ego and its desires. You are no longer deprived. You are full of our love and light. Take no concern of the body, which is deteriorating as it should. You will gladly leave the body when the time comes. You ask for healing, and you know that anything is possible; but at this time of your life, there are more important things for you to do rather than beg for healing. Your soul needs no healing. The body is just a vehicle for learning. Live with soul consciousness, not body consciousness. Begin letting go of the body and its aches and pains. They are of no consequence. Your focus must move beyond the body and its complaints. You were chosen as a vehicle for soul power. Take no heed of what the body is experiencing. Treat it well, but don't focus on it. We have told you this many times before. As your body deteriorates, your focus on soul must grow stronger so that when your time comes, you will be ready to release the body. You will not cling to it. Each of us once had a body.

Your work with those people who look to you

can continue, but don't expect too much of them. Your real work is hidden. It is to express love and light. Your love will heal souls and bodies. When you are able to love yourself as we love you, your body will be healed as well. It will be healed by love, not by your efforts to heal it. Your body has served you well despite the fact that you have created all of its problems. Now is the time to love it and show it gratitude. That is all for now. Thanks for responding to our call.

We directed you to replay the "Transformations of Myth through Time" so that you will be better able to interpret what we will be preparing you for. We need you to have different ways of understanding the experiences of transcendent reality. You must become more comfortable in the transcendental so that when you leave the body this time, you will have no resistance to the death of the body, which is only the vehicle you needed on earth. You are a nine, having completed this cycle of incarnations.

I showed all of the Joseph Campbell video tapes to my mythology class.[4]

For the past two days, I have been so closely linked with the Monad that I am barely aware of the boundaries of my physical body. Last night, only the Monad existed, no nagging pain, no thoughts, and no body. Consciousness alone remained.

So glad you recognized my vibration. You

just prayed to have me, your Monad, take over the direction of your life. Did you really mean it? Well, then let's get started. Every time you question the rightness of an action, call upon me. Ask, "Should I do this?" Then listen to my prompting. Timing is of the essence.

Your compulsive eating is not as much of a problem as it once was. You are more controlled but still have a way to go. Your ego is directing you, not me, your Monad. Once you begin to follow my lead, your life will be more balanced.

I asked, "Was I Saint Catherine of Siena?"

This is a question of your ego, but yes, you were. Don't let it go to your head. You are a long way from your goal of perfection.

You have made many mistakes in this incarnation, but you chose a very difficult path this time around. There were all kinds of obstacles that weren't present in many former lives.

"Can you reveal any other lives that I have not found in regressions?" I asked.

Yes, but they are not important for you to know. You have uncovered some, but you have lived hundreds. I will answer before you ask; your book will be published. Just call upon me for

whatever you need, because as you requested,
I, your larger self, will be available whenever
you need me. Good-bye for now.

My eyes highlight the words I read in gold.

Gerald Heard writes that:

> Intensity of light indicates and expansion of
> consciousness.[5]

October 29, 2008

I intended to end my entries in September of this year, but today, I am literally and figuratively beside myself, holding on to consciousness by a thread, barely able to maintain self-awareness. The realization that my masters, Jesus, Koot Hoomi, and Ramana Maharshi, and I are one is becoming palpable. Everything else is meaningless. Today, I planned to go to a meeting, join friends for lunch, and conduct my class, but I would rather remain here, united with all that is. However, I did manage to get dressed with total focus, though I had no interest in what was happening. Now, as I sit here typing, physical reality is drifting away again, and I am alienated from this body, a stranger difficult to control.

November 2, 2008

Since Wednesday, sudden moments of extreme weakness that are followed by powerful trembling are a prelude to spirit taking control and distancing me from the ego or lesser self that has been in control for most of my life.

It is 4:41 AM, Sunday, and I am sitting at the computer, trying to ignore the trembling that is happening every few seconds. Ordinarily, I would be scared, but the voices say, "Fear not." And after years of doubting, I accept the guidance of those assigned to sponsor my spiritual evolution without reservation. Although the persistent shaking makes typing difficult, I choose to continue doing what I consider an important job, finishing this book. The only relief I get from the tremors is when I sleep. However, when thirst or a dry mouth requires quenching, the trembling starts, making the simple act of taking a gulp of water from the bottle beside my bed quite difficult.

Whenever I'm not attending to necessary and mundane activities, the tremors resume their work of emptying me of all thoughts, desires, and regrets. From time to time for the past week, the body gets my attention with an ache, a cough, a sneeze, or some other necessary function, but otherwise, I'm a blank, with the exception of my old refrain, "What is happening?" which I can't seem to release.

This is the day of the presidential election, and strangely enough, I no longer care who wins. At this particular moment, my interest in everything worldly is gone.

Recently, I was contacted by a guide named Natalie who reminded me of the times she helped me avoid disaster.

I was coming off the Pasadena Freeway at night when the command, "Slow down!" pierced my consciousness. The exit was at a 90 degree angle from the freeway, so it was impossible to see ahead. I slowed down—thank goodness—because there was a stalled car in my path, and I definitely would have hit it.

She also reminded me of the time that a man was following me. It was raining. I was carrying a purse, an umbrella, and clothing for a friend who was being released from the hospital. I noticed a man holding a multicolored umbrella passing me, but he was going in the opposite direction A few moments later, he passed me again, this time inside the building as I waited for the elevator. He was out of sight when the elevator doors opened, but he suddenly appeared, thrusting himself into the elevator with me. As I was busy talking myself out of being afraid, a command screaming "Get out *now!*" mobilized me, and I burst out of the elevator just as the doors closed behind me, leaving the man inside. Well, that could have been Natalie screaming, because it wasn't me.

She reminded me of one warning I did not heed: "Do not enter this woman's (my mother) womb." That really stretched the imagination, but I wished I had listened. When I asked Natalie to defend that preposterous claim, she left without responding.

As I wondered about the experience, I heard, "*Guides and angels act like policemen and firemen to protect you.*"

We mystics and postmodern, spiritual leaders must claim the right to speak out against the limiting ego-centric consciousness that has jeopardized all life on this planet. We must share our visions and inner realities with others so that they also will look into their hearts and souls to find untapped transcendent, transpersonal, and metaphysical realities. Together, we will form a legion of co-creators to birth a new spirituality that brings us in accord with nature and the divine, universal, creative force.

As Abraham Maslow declared:

> You will either step forward into growth or you will
> step back into safety.

November 21, 2008

As I tried to remember how I felt during the many life-changing, ecstatic moments, I longed to leave my aching, aging body behind to once again explore other dimensions of transcendent reality.

This morning, despite the aches and pains of a declining body, I am experiencing the exuberance of youth, and if I could, I would jump for joy. As I look about the room, I bow in reverential gratitude to each of the images of my spiritual Masters: Jesus, Master K. H., my Chinese Master, Buddha, Green Tara, and my beloved Master, Sri Ramana Maharshi. Boundlessly grateful, I am glad to be alive.

Although my mystical experiences probably will continue, because I am a work in progress, I must end this book sometime. Why not now while I am filled to the brim with appreciation for those who have instructed and graced me?

I hope that I have given you an enticing peek into another level of reality available to all who have the desire and the will to explore the depth and profundity of his or her own being.

Self-consciousness is not an end but a phase in the development of consciousness.[6]

October 10, 2009

We are pleased that you are remaining thoughtless as often as possible. Your Master R. M. will allow you to promote your book by using his name. Perhaps you could get approval from the ashram to use his picture.

Dear child, We are pleased with the progress you have made in mind-clearing. Our hope is that you will be able to accept the healing we are sending you. Once again, we warn you to stop focusing on what is wrong with your physical body and accept our messages of perfect health. If you cling to thoughts of ill health, that is what you will have; if you cling to thoughts of vigor and good health, that is what you will have. You have had many examples of healing. Healing does not take time. It is spontaneous.

January 9, 2010

Divest thyself of the beliefs of ordinary humanity. Do not be hampered by the habits of mind that are common to others. You are not to be confined by the false beliefs of mankind, be they ideas like how long you should sleep or the belief of the infirmities of age or even pain. You are a new creature, and you will live by new beliefs about your true nature. Thousands of years of the beliefs of mankind must be shed. Stand guard. Be aware of every thought and know that you are to accept only the thoughts that we plant in your mind. Every thought of limitation must be extinguished. You have climbed to another level in your ascent to us. Your masterhood is closer. You just had a limiting thought. You doubted what we just predicted because you see yourself as limited. You are only limited by your beliefs. This is the transmission your Monad has been waiting for. She is the wise one. Listen to her. Your gifts will be enhanced. The clairvoyance and healing powers will be increased as you shed the belief in limitation. Fear not. You will be able to do whatever is required of you. Take heart. The book will reach those who are ready for its message. Whatever you wish for is yours. We trust that you will wish for things that are already yours from our perspective. You ask if this transmission should be included in the book, and we say yes. But it is up to you.

You have been magnetized to attract to you negative beings. You are drawing them not because you are like them but because like a magnet, you are attracting the opposite polarity. This is not the first incarnation in which you have chosen this work. Your path has not always been straight; but you are now headed in the right direction, and you will complete your journey in this lifetime, having achieved what you came to do. We love and appreciate your willingness to accept difficult assignments.

January 10, 2010

The following is a message for humanity from Jesus:

I want to emphasize that there needs to be a change in consciousness in order to save your planet. The time has come for your transformation from ego selfishness to soul selflessness. The ego has served its purpose. It is time to bring the soul forward and place it in control. The destructive forces you have unleashed are almost beyond repair. Humanity must realize that they are part of the planet and whatever happens to one happens to all—that includes other species, animals and plants. A change in consciousness is the prerequisite for your survival. What you do to others you do to me and to yourselves. We are all one. The ascended masters, who were once in physical bodies, understand your false identification with matter. Matter is the condensation or crystallization of energy—that is all it is. In the future, if there is a future, you will have to realize that all forms of life are valuable and depend on one another.

You have polluted the air you breathe and the waters you drink, and the repercussions are well beyond your understanding. Your thought forms, the source of pollution, affect more than your planet. If you are to survive, you will have to make some drastic changes in the patterns of your thought. Planet Earth was created as an experiment. It was to become a holy planet. Those of us who watch over you are unhappy with the results of that experiment. However, we are still hoping that enough prototypes will be able to reverse and repair the damage.

February 3, 2010

Dearly beloved,

We have warned humanity of the dangerous direction you have taken with your self-centeredness. Now we want to offer you hope. Thanks to the Internet and the World Wide Web, people of like mind have been able to come together to share ideas. Some of these ideas have been negative, but the preponderance has been positive. Humanity is beginning to realize their brotherhood. The catastrophes created by the misguided and those that are natural are bringing people together and making them recognize that the separation they have created between religions, nations, cultures, and each other are of their own creation. Humanity lives *on one small planet in an infinite and growing cosmos. Reach out to each other. Recognize your oneness without having to be motivated by disaster. Keep your thoughts positive and loving or at least compassionate and empathetic. We know that the future seems dark and foreboding, but you can create a brighter and happier future with the power of your thoughts. Be kind to yourselves and to each other, and keep your thoughts positive despite appearances.*

I asked my masters and guides if they had anything more to say. They answered with the following:

We want to thank Renee for working so hard to complete the book. We also want to thank those who have read the book. And we especially want to thank those who have taken our teachings to heart.

Afterword

Today, my focus is no longer on self-development but on the evolution of consciousness of humanity.

Until recently I thought that I had no community of like-minded thinkers, but now I know that there are many of you out there and that the numbers are growing.

I want to thank those individuals and groups that have kept me from feeling alone. They include the following: The Institute of Noetic Sciences, Andrew Cohen, Ken Wilber, Barbara Marx Hubbard, and a growing number of others who are creating a worldwide network of passionate co-creative evolutionaries.

Endnotes

Figure 1: The sayings linked to the symbols came much later. I don't know whether they came as messages or if I read them someplace.

Figure 2: A five and a six pointed star.

Introduction

1. Michel Conge, "Facing Mr. Gurdjieff," in *Gurdjieff, Essays*

and Reflections on the Man and his Teaching, ed. Jacob Needleman and George Baker (New York: Continuum Publishing Co., 1998), 360.

2. Rumi, *The Essential Rumi,* Translated by Coleman Barks. (San Francisco: Harper, 1995).

Chapter 1

1. Jean Houston, *Search for the Beloved* (New York: Tarcher/ Putnam, 1997), 96.

2. Manly Hall, personal notes from Lecture 271, *The Third Eye of the Soul,* Philosophical Research Society, Los Angeles, 1981.

3. Aurobindo, *The Life Divine* (New York: Greystone Press, 1949), 818-19.

Chapter 2

1. Deepak Chopra, *Quantum Healing* (New York: Bantam Books, 1990), 174.

2. Jiddu Krishnamurti, *Krishnamurti's Notebook* (Ojai, CA: Krishnamurti Publications of America, 1976).

3. Gerald Heard, *Pain, Sex and Time* (Rhinebeck, NY: Monkfish Book Publishing Co., 2004), 136.

4. Eckhart Tolle, *The Power of Now* (Novato, CA: New World Library, 1999), 43.

Chapter 3

No notes

Chapter 4

1. Paul Twitchell, *Dialogues with the Master* (Menlo Park, CA: Illuminated Way Press, 1970), 17.

2. Baha'u'llah, in *Mystics, Masters, Saints and Sages*, ed. RobertUllman and Judyth Reichenberg (Berkeley, CA: Conari Press, 2001), 92.

3. Norman Friedman, *Bridging Science and Spirit* (Boston, MA: Red Wheel Weiser, 1986), 274 -75.

4. S. Abhayananda, *History of Mysticism* (Olympia, WA: Atma Books, 1996), 7.

5. Ken Wilber, *Integral Spirituality* (Boston, MA: Shambhala Publication, 2006), 95.

6. B. Magee, *Philosophy of Schopenhauer* (New York: Oxford University Press, 1997).

7. Hall, personal notes from Lecture 271.

8. Ervin Lazlo, *Shift in Action* (Petaluma, CA: Institute of Noetic Sciences, Teleseminar, 2008).

9. S. Abhayananda, *The Supreme Self* (NY: O Books, 2005), 36.

10. David Bohm, in *Mysticism and Science*, ed. S. Abhayananda (Olympia, WA: Atma Books, 1996), 41.

11. Ramakrishna, in *Mystics, Masters, Saints and Sages*, Ullman, 93.

12. Hall, personal notes from Lecture 271.

13. Alfred Tennyson, in William James, *Varieties of Religious Experiences* (New York: The Modern Library, 1902), 374.

14. Paramahansa Yogananda, in *Mystics, Masters, Saints and Sages*, Ullman, 118.

15. Heard, *Pain, Sex and Time*, 155.

16. Gendun Gyatso Palzangpo, in *Mystics, Masters, Saints and*

Sages, Ullman, 60.

Chapter 5

1. Barbara Marx Hubbard, *Revelation* (Mill Valley, CA: Nataraj Publishing Co., 1995), 219.

2. J.N. Findlay, "The Ascent to the Absolute: Metaphysical Papers and Lectures," Muirhead Library of Philosophy (New York: Allen & Unwin, 1970).

3. Saint Symeon, quoted from *The Hero with a Thousand Faces,* ed. Joseph Campbell (Princeton, NJ: Princeton University Press, 1949), 39.

4. Ramakrishna, quoted from *History of Mysticism,* Abhayananda, 386.

5. Turkom Saraydarian, *The Magnet of Life: A Psychological Key to the Inner Man* (Agoura, CA: Aquarian Educational Group, 1968), 54.

6 Hakuin, in Mystics, Masters, Saints and Sages, Ullman, 73

Chapter 6

1. Bernie S. Seigel, "A Way of Healing," in *Parabola,* 22, 4 (1997), 59.

2. Abhayananda, *History of Mysticism,* 7.

3. Catherine of Siena, in *Mystics, Masters, Saints and Sages,* 41.

4. Ibid., 37–45.

Chapter 7

1. Jaques Choisnel, "An Unfinished Creation: A Christian Understanding of Gurdjieff's Teachings," ed. Jacob Needleman and George Baker, *Gurdjieff* (New York: Continuum Publishing Co., 1998), 205.

2. *Holy Bible*, Authorized (King James) Version: Matt. 6:28.

3. Peace Pilgrim, in *Mystics, Masters, Saints and Sages*, Ullman, 147.

4. Jean Houston, *The Hero and the Goddess* (New York: Ballantine Books, 1984), 73.

5. Dag Hammarskjold, *Markings* (New York: Alfred A. Knopf, 1964), 166.

Chapter 8

1. Ken Wilber, *Spectrum of Consciousness* (Wheaton, IL: Quest Books, 1977), 22.

2. Paul Twitchell, *Dialogues with the Master* (Menlo Park, CA: Illuminated Way Press, 1970), 38.

3. Alice Bailey, *Letters on Occult Meditation* (New York: Lucis Publishing Company, 1974), 173-74.

Chapter 9

1. Marilyn Schlitz, et al., *Living Deeply: The Art & Science of Transformation in Everyday Life* (Oakland, CA: New Harbinger Publications and Noetic Books, 2007), 109.

2. K. G. Durckheim, "The Call for the Master," *Parabola*, 14, 1 (1989), 6.

3. Eliade Mircea, *Rites and Symbols of Initiation* (New York:

Harper Torchbooks, 1958), 128.

4. Robert Adams, in *Mystics, Masters, Saints and Sages*, Ullman, 191.

Chapter 10

1. Yogi Ramacharaka, *The Spirit of the Upanishads* (Chicago: Yogi Publication Society, 1907), 24.

2. Alice Bailey, *Esoteric Psychology 11* (New York: Lucis, 1964), 791, Index (difficulties and diseases of the mystic).

3. Twitchell, *Dialogues*, 33.

4. Alice Bailey, *Initiation, Human and Solar* (New York: Lucis, 1977), 10.

5. John White, *The Meeting of Science and Spirit* (New York: Paragon House, 1990), 14.

6. Deepa Kodikal, in *Mystics, Masters, Saints and Sages*, Ullman, 209.

7. Hall, personal notes from Lecture 271.

8. Abraham Abulafia, in *Mystics, Masters, Saints and Sages*, 32.

9. A. H. Almaas, quoted from *A Mythic Life*, Jean Houston (San Francisco: Harper Collins Publishing, 1996) 125.

10. Ibid., 127.

11. Gregg Braden, audio book: *Walking Between the Worlds*, (Bloomfield, Colorado: Conscious Wave, Inc.)

Chapter 11

No Notes

Chapter 12

1.   Marilyn Schlitz, *Living Deeply*, 109.

2.   Joseph Campbell, *The Inner Reaches of Outer Space*, (New York: Harper & Row, 1986), 35–8.

3.   Manly Hall, *The Secret Teachings of All Ages* (Los Angeles: Philosophical Research Society, Inc., 1978), 69.

4.   Manly Hall, *Self-Unfoldment* by Disciplines of Realization (Los Angeles: The Philosophical Research Society, Inc., 1996), 105.

5.   Eliezer Shore, "The Temple of Amount," *Parabola* 24, 3 (1999), 13.

6.   P. D. Ouspensky, "The One and the Many," *Parabola,* ibid., 61.

7.   Titus Burkhardt, "Symbolism of the Mirror," *Parabola,* ibid., 83.

8.   John Curtis Gowan, *Trance, Art and Creativity* (Buffalo, NY: State University College, 1975), 255.

9.   Lucinda Vardey, *God in All Worlds: An Anthology of Contemporary Spiritual Writing* (New York: Pantheon Books, 1995), 126.

10. Robert W. Godwin, *One Cosmos under God* (St Paul, MN: Paragon House, 2004), 39.

11. John Cornwell, *The Hiding Places of God* (New York: Warner Books, 1991), 98.

12. Eliade Mircea, *Rites and Symbols*, 86.

Chapter 13

1.   "Signs of Agni Yoga," *Fiery World 1* (New York: Agni Yoga Society Inc., 1933), 243.

2. Alice Bailey, *Letters on Occult Meditation*, 274.

3. Gerald Heard, *Pain, Sex and Time* (Rhinebeck, NY: Monkfish Book Publishing Co., 2004), 167.

Chapter 14

1. Alice Bailey, *Treatise on Cosmic Fire* (Albany, NY: Fort Orange Press, 1974), 82.

2. Gopi Krishna, in *Mystics, Masters, Saints and Sages*, Ullman, 157–8.

3. Ibid., 101.

4. Isaac Bentov, *Stalking the Wild Pendulum* (New York: Dutton, 1977), 174.

5. Alice Bailey, *Telepathy* (New York: Lucis, 1974), 26.

6. Alice Bailey, *Initiation Human and Solar* (New York: Lucis, 1974), 163.

7. Ramana Maharshi, *The Spiritual Teachings of Ramana Maharshi* (Tiruvannamali, India: Ramanasraman, 2004).

8. T. M. R. Mahadevan, *Ramana Maharshi the Sage of Arunacala* (London: Mandala Books, 1977).

9. Sir John Woodroffe, quoted from *The Inner Reaches of Outer Space*. Joseph Campbell, 102.

10. Henry David Thoreau, quoted from *The Journal of Henry David Thoreau,* ed. Bradford Torrey and Francis H. Allen (New York: Dover Publication, Inc., 1906).

11. Heard, *Pain, Sex and Time*, 167.

12. Aurobindo, *Life Divine*, 819.

13. Hall, Lecture 271.

14. Shafica Karagulla and Viola Petitt, *Through the Curtain* (Sunol, CA: DAEL Crystal Co., 1983), 141.

Chapter 15

1. Ghazali, *Mysticism in the World's Religions,* ed. Jeoffrey Parinder (Oxford University Press, 1976), 137.

2. Titus Burkhardt, "Symbolism of the Mirror," *Parabola,* 24, 2 (1999), 84.

3. Abhayananda, *The History of Mysticism,* 41.

4. Thomas Moore, "Neither Here nor There," *Parabola,* 25, 1 (2000), 34.

5. Jessica Woodroffe, in *The Meeting of East and West,* ed. F. S. C. Northrop (New York: Macmillan, 1946), 36.

Chapter 16

1. Alice Bailey, *Esoteric Psychology 11* (New York: Lucis, 1974), 619.

2. Nietzsche, www.*Brainy Quotes.*

3. P. D. Ouspensky, "The One and the Many," *Parabola,* (1999), Vol. 24, 3, 59.

4. Surkumar Ghose, *Mystic and Society* (New York: Sisirkumar Asia Publishing House, 1968), 45.

5. Aurobindo, *Life Divine,* 824.

6. Joseph Campbell, *The Power of Myth,* interviewed by Bill Moyers for Public TV.

7. Helen Blavatsky, in *The Chakras,* ed. C. W. Leadbeater (Wheaton, IL: Theosophical Publishing House, 1973), 31.

8. Lester Levinson, in *Mystics, Masters, Saints, and Sages,* Ullman, 171.

9. Hazrat Inayat Khan, *Sufi Teaching* (New Lebanon, NY: Omega Publications, 1991), 135.

Chapter 17

1. Malcom Muggeridge, interviewed by William F. Buckley, (Los Angeles: KCET, December 27, 1997).

Chapter 18

1. Ken Wilber, *Spectrum of Consciousness*, 22.

Chapter 19

2. Krishnamurti, in *Mystics, Masters, Saints and Sages*, Ullman, 137.

3. Alice Bailey, *Externalization of the Hierarchy* (Lucis), 600–61.

4. Aurobindo, *Life Divine*, 826.

5. Bailey, *Letters on Occult Meditation*, 130–8.

Chapter 20

1. Hall, *Self-Unfoldment*, 139.

2. Ibid., 141.

3. Krishnamurti, *Notebook*.

4. Bentov, *Stalking the Wild Pendulum*, 212.

5. Houston, *Search for the Beloved*, 204.

Chapter 21

1. Advadhut Gita in *History of Mysticism*, 204.

Chapter 22

1. Aurobindo, *Life Divine*, 829.

2. Heard, *Pain, Sex and Time*, 132.

3. Ibid., 174.

Chapter 23

1. Ken Wilber, *Sex, Ecology, Spirituality: The Spirit of Evolution*, (Boston & London, 2000), 501.

2. Heard, *Pain, Sex and Time*, 46.

3. Rumi, *The Essential Rumi*.

4. Rumi, *The Essential Rumi*.

5. Peter A. Kwasniewski, "Wise and Foolish Virgins," *Parabola*, 23, 2 (1998), 22.

6. Ibid., 28.

7. *Bhagavad Gita*, trans. S. Radhakrishnan (India: Blackie & Son, 1977), 18–66, 378.

8. Andrew Cohen, *EnlightenNext* magazine, March–May, 2009, 43.

Chapter 24

No Notes

Chapter 25

1. Evelyn Underhill, *Mysticism* (Cleveland, OH: Meridian Books, 1955), 157.

2. Needleman, *Gurdjieff,* 83.

3. Pir Vilay Inayat Khan, *Search of the Hidden Treasure* (New York: Tarcher/Putnam, 2003), 52.

4. David R. Hawkins, *Reality and Subjectivity* (West Sedona, AZ: Veritas Publishing, 2003).

Chapter 26

1. Mara Freeman, "Enchanted Beasts and Faerie Women, Celtic Symbols of the Soul," *Parabola,* 24, 3 (1999), 25.

2. Aurobindo, *Life Divine*, 929.

3. Hall, *Self-Unfoldment,* 27.

4. Thomas Moore, " Neither Here nor There" *Parabola,* "Threshold," 25, 1 (2000), 37.

Chapter 27

1. Richard Bucke, *Cosmic Consciousness* (New York: Dutton, 1969).

2. Dean Radin, "A Quantum View of the World," *Shift in Action* (Web, Institute of Noetic Sciences 2009), personal notes.

3. "The Three Faces of God," *Integral Spirituality* (Web. discussion between Andrew Cohen and Ken Wilber 2009), personal notes.

4. Joseph Campbell, "The World of Joseph Campbell," *Transformations of Myth through Time* (Public Media Videos, USA, 800.262.8600, 1989).

5. Heard, *Pain, Sex and Time,* 84.

6. Ibid., 174.

Glossary

Agni: Vedic god of fire.

Agnostic: One who believes that any existence of ultimate reality (God) is unknown.

Akashic Records: Scenic representations of every action, sentiment, and thought since the beginning of the world.

Ambrosia: Food of the gods in Greek mythology.

Antakarana: The silver chord that connects lower and higher vehicles; the soul and spirit with the physical body and the ego.

Aquarian Epoch: The era of the world, according to occult teachings, that began in March, 1948, and is to last two thousand years.

Aspirant: A student of esoteric philosophy with a desire to become a disciple.

Astral Body: A replica of the physical body but of more subtle substance.

Astral Projection: The separation of the astral from the physical body, visiting other localities. The adept or Master can command his or her astral body to go any place.

Audition: The hearing of voices with the physical auditory equipment (e.g., ears).

AUM: In Hinduism, it is the sacred sound of creation, said to contain all other sounds, and used as a mantra.

Aura: A psychic effluvium that emanates from the physical body that can be brilliant, multicolored, or dull, according to the character of the person or thing. Esoterically, it is composed of electro-vital and electro-mental magnetism, visible only to psychics and very young children.

Automatic Painting: The production of paintings by a medium without the control of his conscious self.

Automatic Speech: The production of a medium speaking without the control of his conscious self.

Automatic Writing: The production of script by a medium without the control of his conscious self.

Bodhisattva: Sanskrit for existence in wisdom. One who renounces eternal peace in nirvana and pledges to incarnate until all sentient beings have achieved the same.

Bhagavad Gita: Sanskrit for "Song of the Divine One." The title of an epic poem inserted in the Mahabharata, containing a dialogue between Arjuna and Krishna.

Biolocation: The phenomenon in which the body occupies or seems to be present in two places simultaneously.

Brother: An initiate who works toward the accomplishment of his task in all incarnations.

Caduceus: The wand of Hermes or Mercury, the messenger of the gods. A rod with two serpents entwined around it with two wings at the top.

Causal Body: The vehicle of the spirit.

Chakra: A sense organ of the ethereal body, visible only to clairvoyants.

Chela: Sanskrit for disciple.

Color Awareness: According to occult teachings, color has a tremendous influence on the human mind and body. In learning the mastery of color, man can become the master of his thought and the ruler of his destiny.

Creme, Benjamin: He forecast that Jesus would declare Himself to be incarnated on June 21, 1982. It did not happen.

Dark Night: A depression brought about by a sense of having lost spiritual contact.

Deva: Elemental nature spirit.

Disciple: Follower of a school or a teacher.

Ego: Personality.

Elohim: One of the Hebrew names for God.

Esoteric: Secret, not accessible to the uninitiated.

Extrasensory Perception (ESP): A term coined by Dr. J. B. Rhine of Duke University. It is a response to an external event not presented to any known sense.

Gemini: Third sign of the zodiac (May 21 to June 20).

Gnome: Spirit of the earth, visible only to those who have inner sight.

Gross Body: The physical body.

Hierophant: Greek for demonstrator of sacred matters; the initiator into esoteric knowledge.

Incarnation: The assumption of a physical body.

Krishna: The eighth avatar (reincarnation of Vishnu) of Hindu mythology. His teachings are recorded in the Bhagavad Gita.

Kundalini: Energy that lies dormant at the base of the spine until activated. Then it is channeled upward through the chakras as one works toward spiritual perfection.

Levitation: The raising of the human body without any visible means, contrary to the law of gravitation.

Maharshi: Great sage who discloses a path to realization.

Mahatma: Great soul.

Mantra: An incantation.

Metaphysics: The philosophical theory of reality; the science of obscure and occult mysteries.

Monad: The immortal part of man that lives on in successive reincarnations.

Nirvana: The extinction of individuality, without a loss of consciousness.

Occult: Hidden from the uninitiated.

Paranormal: Supernatural.

Reincarnation: Rebirth of the divine essence (soul) in a new body.

Rune: Any character from an ancient Germanic alphabet. Each rune has its own magical significance.

Shakti: The energy of kundalini.

Shambhala: The highest spiritual center on the planet, a mystical place thought to be in Northern Tibet where enlightened masters reside.

Shiva: Hindu god of destruction.

Stigmata: Wounds of the crucifixion that have appeared on the bodies of mystics.

Subtle Body: The part of an individual that survives death and is reborn.

Taurus: The second sign of the Zodiac (April 21 to May 20).

Telepathy: Transmission of thoughts.

Third Eye: Ajna center enables a living human to see the astral world. It is identified with the pineal gland.

Trance: A state of apparent unconsciousness.

Upanishads: Books that contain the esoteric wisdom of Vedanta, Hindu philosophy.

Vishnu: One of the three gods of the Hindu trinity.

Wesak: The three full-moon festivals (Aires, Taurus, and Gemini) offer humanity an opportunity to approach divinity. At the time of Wesak, during the full moon of Taurus, two powerful streams of energy—one from the Buddha, the other from the Christ—are fused, and with the help of the world servers, rains down upon the earth.